I0429449

UNCOMMON SENSE

I. ON THE NATURE OF OUR PROBLEM

"Some writers have so confounded society with government, as to leave little or no distinction between them ... Society is produced by our wants, & government by our wickedness; the former produces happiness positively by uniting our affections, the latter negatively by restraining our vices." - Thomas Paine, Common Sense, Chapter I

We have believed a lie. The lie is this: that there is a Better Sort of People, who are entitled to the power to tell the rest of us what to do, for the sake of the Greater Good. This lie has gone by many names, as variations of it have infected governments down through history. In America, it is currently called Liberalism, or Progressivism, or even Democratic Socialism. Those who believe in this lie are convinced that it is "rule by the best", which is the literal meaning of "aristocracy". But, to coin a word, it would be more accurate to call it "diaseiocracy" (dee-as-i'-o-cra-cee), or "rule by intimidation" -- literally, "rule by shake-down". Because it is not merely a collection of policy preferences, nor just a political strategy, but a philosophical system for justifying the acquisition & exercise of power.

In the earliest governments, the lie was sold on the basis that the King was a god personified -- so we must submit. Disobedience was heresy. When that would no longer sell, the pitch shifted to the "divine right of kings". The monarch, if not a god, was heaven's authority on earth -- so we must submit. When that couldn't be taken seriously anymore, the idea of the aristocracy was lifted up. The aristocrats weren't divine, but they were "bred to rule" -- so we must submit. When inbreeding undermined that idea, the sell shifted to racism -- the "white man's burden". From the American South to the Indian Subcontinent, dominion was justified by the need to "civilize the savages" -- so we must

> **Which are stronger, societies based on coercion, or those based on freedom?**

all submit. After experience revealed racism to be ridiculous, science was enlisted to prop up the right to rule. Darwin's revelation of evolution allowed crude racism to be upgraded to scientific racism, to be rationally implemented through abortion, eugenics & euthanasia. Since

copyright 2016 © J. M. Payne

the power was being exercised scientifically --- <u>we must submit</u>. More recently, class warfare & Marx's historical dialectic were developed to justify revolutionary collectivization (& just incidentally produce the protracted miseries of Communism.) To resist the Revolution was to be on the wrong side of history; a brave new world was being built -- <u>so we must certainly submit</u>.

The attempts to build this brave new world are why the history of the 20th century was written in fire & blood. Those fires were set & that blood was shed to answer this question: Which are stronger, societies based on coercion, or those based on freedom? Fascists, Nazis & Communists were all confident that the undisciplined, soft, independent, noisy, disorganized, lovers of liberty would fall before their goose-stepping legions. But when the dust settled & the smoke cleared, it was Liberty standing tall on the ashes of the tyrannies.

The Sales Pitch

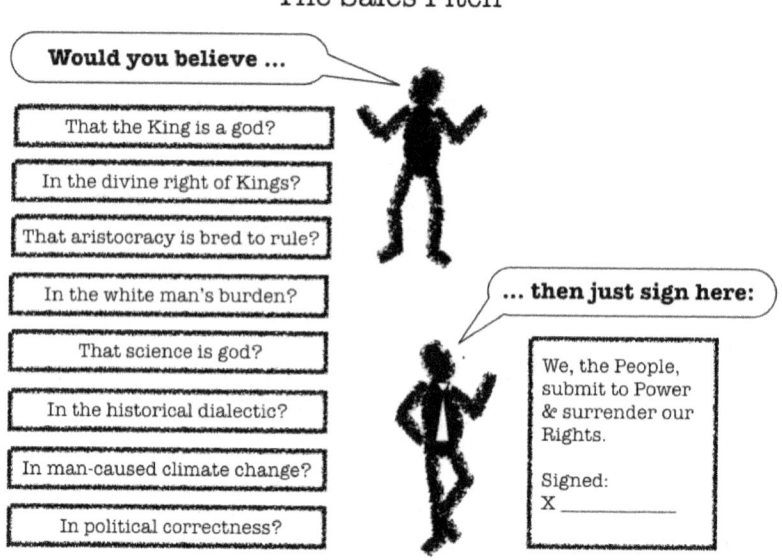

The front end is whatever sounds good, but the back end is always the same: <u>we must submit</u>.

So, the verdict is in. Freedom is stronger than coercion. But Liberals still bitterly cling to the idea that the only way to move society forward is through the coercive transformation of society. Perhaps we should sympathize -- imagine for a moment that it was the USSR that was prosperous, happy & a colossus astride the world, & that America was poor, miserable & had fallen apart in 1991. How would that feel? Would we Americans cheerfully admit that the Declaration of Independence was a failure, & happily join the Communist Party?

copyright © 2016 J. M. Payne

The only thing Liberals have left to sell their lie is a loose set of incoherent moralisms called "political correctness". Those who would rule us have gone from styling themselves as gods, to being reduced to whining & nagging. Philosophically, the lie has dried up. Operationally, it is robust, & its roots are deep & extensive. This is largely because it has been established through the world's most successful & pervasive form of tyranny: bureaucracy.

- ☐ Bureaucracy is senseless. The word is derived from "bureau", the French for "desk", & "-cracy", the Greek for "to rule". Isn't it obvious that we ought to be suspicious of a system that literally means to be governed by furniture?

- ☐ Bureaucracy is authoritarian. It exists because an authority declares, "If you want to do X, go to that desk & do what you're told to do." We'll be told to create paperwork to feed the bureaucracy that is telling us what to do. We submit to this because the authority will punish us if we exercise our freedom regarding X without its permission.

- ☐ Bureaucracy is faceless. It provides no personal targets for its victims. In bureaucracy, blame is diffused by procedures; power is hidden by policy. Fighting it is like climbing a mountain of molasses. There is nothing to get a grip on; it flows relentlessly against every movement; it oozes tirelessly over us until we are exhausted & smothered.

That Liberalism has infused government bureaucracy has been established so well by others, that the point need not be belabored here. The intent here is to move our attention from what Liberals say they intend to do with power, & direct it to what they do with that power, because the purpose of any system is what it does. I submit that Liberalism does not produce the promised utopia of peace, justice &

> **Liberals don't seek power because they think that they can really produce the utopia they promise; they seek power because they are controlled by the need to control us.**

equality, because that is not its purpose. Instead, those accumulating power are driven by an uncontrollable need to control the rest of us. Their handbook, Saul Alinski's "Rules for Radicals", gives detailed instructions on how to acquire power, but offers nothing at all on the purposes for which power should be used. This is because Liberalism is an addiction to power & addiction is its own justification.

copyright 2016 © J. M. Payne

Too much of our political conversation is like a person earnestly explaining the terrible consequences of alcohol abuse to an alcoholic, expecting that he will thereby be persuaded to stop drinking. But, the alcoholic doesn't drink because he <u>thinks</u> he should; he drinks because he <u>feels</u> he must. The need makes itself 1st priority; all other priorities are rescinded.   What we need when dealing with addiction is not persuasion, nor negotiation, but <u>intervention</u>. Addicts & their enablers weave a web of wishful thinking to avoid facing the real problem.   In today's politics, we call this being "moderate", "nuanced", "bipartisan", or "politically correct". This is not hypocrisy, but a form of denial. Some examples:

- ☐ Dividing people into categories is "divisiveness" & bad; but "diversity", which also requires dividing people into categories, is good.

- ☐ "Tobacco must be demonized!" but, "Marijuana must be legalized!"

- ☐ Big corporations raising their prices is "greedy profiteering", but big government's "revenue enhancement" is "courageous statesmanship".

- ☐ We must do everything "for the children" – except protect their right to be born.

- ☐ "The Social Security Trust Fund is the world's safest investment!" but it is required by law to "invest" in I.O.U.'s from the Federal government, which is broke.

- ☐ "Social justice demands that politicians fix income inequality!" Yet history shows that when politicians fix incomes, they make themselves & their cronies "more equal" than the rest of us.

- ☐ "Every American has the right to own a home!" A century ago, to own a home meant to own it outright, not merely to be paying a mortgage. If the roof fell in on us financially, there would still be a roof over our heads, physically. Now, like renters, "owner" must pay to have a place to stay.

- ☐ "We can't legislate outmoded, Victorian sexual morality!" Yet, "We are morally obligated to legislate homosexual marriage as a civil right!"

- ☐ If evolution produced us, then we are simply part of the ecosystem, no different from any other life form. A beehive is as "artificial" as a bank building; Hoover Dam is as "natural" as a beaver dam. So if a species is made extinct by human activity, isn't that just evolution in action?

copyright © 2016 J. M. Payne

- ☐ The 1st Amendment states, "Congress shall make no law respecting an establishment of religion, or prohibiting the free exercise thereof; ... " yet Liberals go to court to flip this restriction on government power to empower government to purge public expressions of faith.

- ☐ Liberals seek to pre-empt ideas they don't like by insisting that any ideas that don't fit into the conceptual box they call "science" are illegitimate. This is "political correctness" wearing a lab coat, which is both unscientific & intolerant.

This addiction to power is as old as government & has gone by many names besides Liberalism. My purpose here is not to critique it, as this has already been done thoroughly, in Mark Levin's "Ameritopia", Rush Limbaugh's "The Way Things Ought to Be", Glenn Beck's "An Inconvenient Book", Mark Levin's "Ameritopia: The Unmaking of America" & many others. The purpose here is simply to undermine the flawed mental model that Liberalism is rational, modern, progressive & scientific.   We do this by applying a rule of human behavior: "The purpose of a system is what is does".   Lay aside the sales pitch that Liberalism is the best way to show compassion to the poor, right the wrongs of history, save the children, & save the planet; what is it that

> **"Render to Caesar that which is Caesar's ... but Liberalism says that _everything_ is Caesar's.**

they are, in fact, doing?   They are converting our government into a machine for the comprehensive control of society. The machine decides where our kids should go to school; determines our retirement benefits; controls our access to medical care; & grows by consuming our liberties. Jesus of Nazareth commanded, "Render to Caesar that which is Caesar's, & to God that which is God's", but Liberalism says that _everything_ is Caesar's. They say it's for the Greater Good, but I submit that it is an addiction to control.

There is nothing new in this.   Escaped slave Frederick Douglass recounted in his "Narrative of the Life of Frederick Douglass an American Slave", that his master

> "... exhorted me to content myself & be obedient. He told me, if I would be happy, I must lay out no plans for the future. He said, if I behaved myself properly, he would take care of me.   Indeed, he advised me to complete thoughtlessness of the future, & taught me to depend solely upon him for happiness... But in spite of him, & even in spite

copyright 2016 © J. M. Payne

of myself, I continued to think … about the injustice of my enslavement & the means of escape."

This man, born into slavery, loved liberty enough to risk losing it all in the attempt to gain freedom. If we who claim to love liberty lose it to those love power, it will not be because our opponents outsmart us, outnumber us, outspend us, or out-organize us. It comes down to this: Do we love liberty more than they love power? This time could be the last stand for Liberty, or for the great lie of Liberalism. It is a question of what we faith, & knowing what we believe requires clear thinking.

copyright © 2016 J. M. Payne

II. On Correcting Our Mental Models

"... a long habit of not thinking a thing <u>wrong</u>, gives it a superficial appearance of being <u>right</u>, & raises at 1st a formidable outcry in defense of custom. But the tumult soon subsides." - Thomas Paine, Common Sense, author's introduction

It is impossible to think clearly with bad mental models. As a simple example, consider driving a car to a particular destination. We use a mental model to navigate -- memories, a map, or GPS . If that mental model is well correlated to the real world, we'll likely reach our destination without much difficulty. But if the mental model is flawed because it, or our interpretation of it, is wrong, we're going to get lost. We can admit our error & change direction, & probably get where we want to go. But if we keep driving as if the real world matches our flawed mental model, our trip will end in failure (or a wreck). As Ayn Rand, in "Atlas Shrugged" challenged us: "There are no contradictions. If you find one, check your premises."

So, what's going on in our heads needs to correlate tolerably well with the real world. When we cling to bad mental models, higher intelligence undermines us, because we can better persuade ourselves that correction isn't required. Like adding computational power to a computer with flawed software, we just generate errors faster. We like to cling to dysfunctional mental models because, unlike reality, we can shape them to conform to the curves of our biases. Bad mental models feel good. This is the secret of Liberalism's success in politics, & of its failure in everything else.

Now, building good mental models is hard work. As the perceptive engineer William L. Livingston put it, "Thinking is labor of the highest difficulty & the most unpopular sport in the world." Conservatism works by distilling truths from experience & history, building these into coherent structures, & then conserving that wisdom. One of the more vital of these distillations is in the Declaration of Independence: "We hold these truths to be self-evident, that all men are created equal, that they are endowed by their Creator with certain unalienable Rights, that among these are Life, Liberty & the pursuit of Happiness -- That to secure these rights, Governments are instituted among Men, deriving their just powers from the consent of the governed." The application of these truths in history has led Conservatives to the conviction that freedom, supported by a structure of laws & rights, produces the most happiness for the most people.

The American Way is built on these truths -- a system in which we make our own places in society, based on what we can do, individually & in association. Government's role is to be the structure that secures our

copyright 2016 © J. M. Payne

rights & supports our liberties, not a vast control machine that runs our lives. In contrast, the Liberal Utopia would be a society that has surrendered to the machine. If the Liberal Utopia is true, then the American Way is a lie. If the American Way works, then Liberalism is a dead end. And history has shown that it is freedom that works. We Americans -- a ragtag collection of ex-colonists, populated by all the people the rest of the world didn't want -- have become prosperous, happy & a colossus astride the world.

> **"Thinking is labor of the highest difficulty & the most unpopular sport in the world." - William R. Livingston**

If these words sound odd, alien, unbelievable, even jingoistic, it's because Liberals have carefully conceived & skillfully executed a century long evangelization in the guise of education, propaganda through the press, & advertising sold as entertainment, to shape our mental models to fit their agenda. Listen again to Frederick Douglass: "I have found that, to make a contented slave it is necessary to make a thoughtless one. It is necessary to darken his moral & mental vision, & as far as possible, to annihilate the power of reason. He must be able to detect no inconsistencies in slavery; he must be made to feel that slavery is right ..." This is what is being done to us. The political Party of Liberalism, founded on the slave plantation, has never given up the dream of being our masters. Instead, they have expanded it; formerly they were content to own people of one skin color, now they intend to own us all. So, it's time to erase the old, bad mental models & replace them with ones suitable for the thinking of free citizens.

copyright © 2016 J. M. Payne

BAD MENTAL MODEL

LIBERAL   MODERATE   CONSERVATIVE

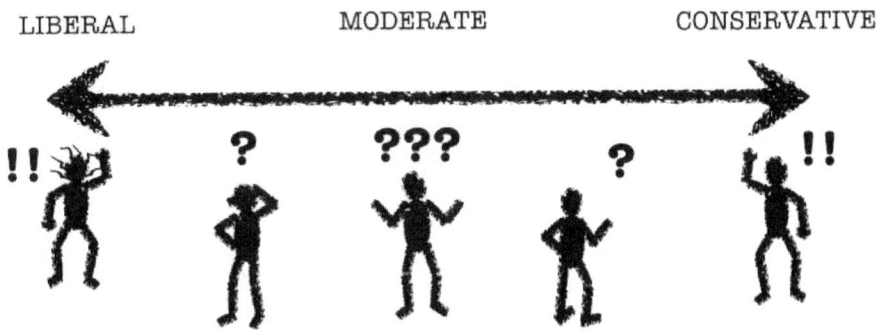

Bad Mental Model: an Arbitrary Spectrum of Positions

Let's begin with the concept of "the political spectrum". Politics is commonly conceived as a spectrum like that in the figure, with Left versus Right & Moderates in between.   It is a sort of ideological smorgasbord, from which we pick & choose what policies we like. Those towards the ends of the spectrum tend to try to fit their choices into an ideological framework, what we call Liberal or Conservative.   The choices of those in the middle tend to flow from personal experience, emotional inclination, or social pressure, instead of ideology. Any given person's positions, of course, will reflect a unique mix of rational & emotional factors. Now, the conventional wisdom is that those in the middle are "moderate" & therefore better than those at the ends, who are "extremists". The "extremists" are assumed to be purists who act out of partisanship or arrogance. The moderates tend to define "best" as the compromise that is least objectionable to the most people.   This approach confuses popularity with viability.   It also requires believing that politicians & lobbyists are disinterestedly pursuing compromise for the Greater Good, & not spinning public opinion from greed for money & lust for power.   We can no longer afford such an inadequate mental model. Government is serious business. Does a sports team take the field with a careless game plan? Would anyone start a business without a carefully thought out business case? Let's not carry this   flawed, linear spectrum model into the arena of politics.

copyright 2016 © J. M. Payne

IMPROVED MENTAL MODEL

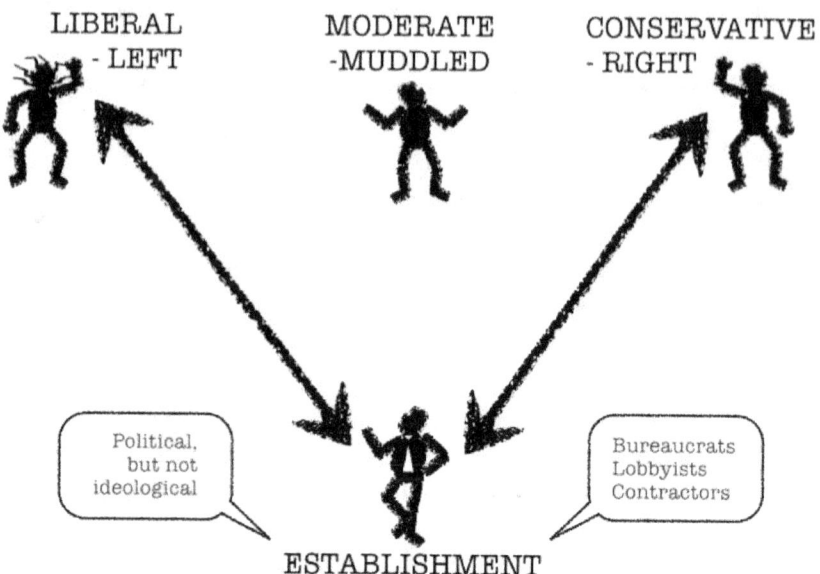

Improved Mental Model: a Three-Cornered Battlefield

I propose that a better model would be a triangular one. A triangle is appropriate because politics is not a 2-sided fight, but a 3-cornered battle, consisting of:

☐ The Left, concentrating political power as a means to the end of controlling our society;

☐ The Right, constraining political power as a means to the end of securing our Liberty;

☐ The Establishment, consolidating political power as an end unto itself.

So, we see that as we move away from the Left & Right corners, we do not necessarily go towards a moderate middle. (And those in the middle tend to be more muddled than moderate anyway.) We tend to go in another, downward direction, towards the bottom corner. This is where those with a great vested interest in politics, but no particular political ideology, gather. This pragmatic corner produces most of the dirtiness in politics. The other, principled corners are the source of most of the silliness in politics.

copyright © 2016 J. M. Payne

That the 3rd corner, the Establishment, is so powerful & yet so often ignored, is the fatal flaw in the spectrum model of politics. Think of bureaucrats whose 1st priority is their budgets; lobbyists who write bills that aren't even read by the legislators who pass them; administrators who aren't particular about the policies being implemented, as long as they're doing the implementing; contractors who contribute on both sides of the aisle, so that they win the business, no matter who wins the election. All these are in the Establishment because they are politically dependent, but philosophically agnostic. They put the dirt into dirty politics, because they will do whatever it takes to win. They may favor policies that are Conservative or Liberal, but these are preferences, not priorities.

POLITICAL AXES

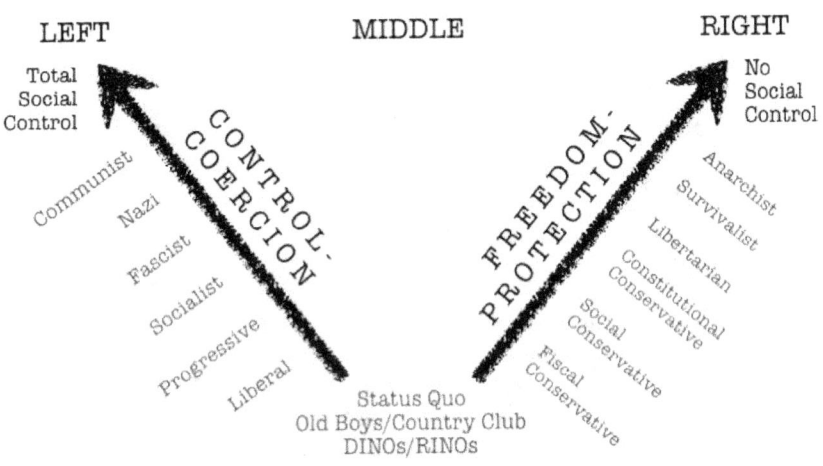

The Left is one axis; the Right is another axis; position along each axis
is determined by how far one is willing to go to achieve that agenda.

Now, let's develop this model a bit further by viewing the left & right sides of our triangle as political axes themselves. On the Left, we have a continuum of coercion, from the mildness of Liberalism, through Socialism & on to the extremes of Communism. People on this axis would march us to their utopia, where everything is a political thing. If it's a forced march, well, they're sure we'll thank them, once we're there. What varies is the level of coercion they're willing to apply. For a Communist, genocide is acceptable, while a Liberal feels sure that nagging (aka, "political correctness") will get us there. On the Right, there is a continuum of freedom, from Fiscal Conservatives who worry about the impact of politics on their pocketbooks, through

copyright 2016 © J. M. Payne

Constitutional Conservatives, on to Anarchists who are convinced that any political structure is anathema. What varies here is how much independence is demanded. This "mind your own business" mentality of the Right protects against the tyranny which is characteristic of the Left, but it also the main reason the Right loses on the political battlefield. At the bottom of our triangle, sits the Establishment: the Old Boys' network & Country Clubbers , with the DINO's (Democrats In Name Only) & RINO's (Republicans In Name Only). What varies among them is who they are willing to throw under the bus to protect the status quo. So, the Left is tempted to control the world, while the Right is tempted to abandon it. We will see that the Establishment is not neutral with respect to these temptations.

POLITICAL IDEOLOGIES

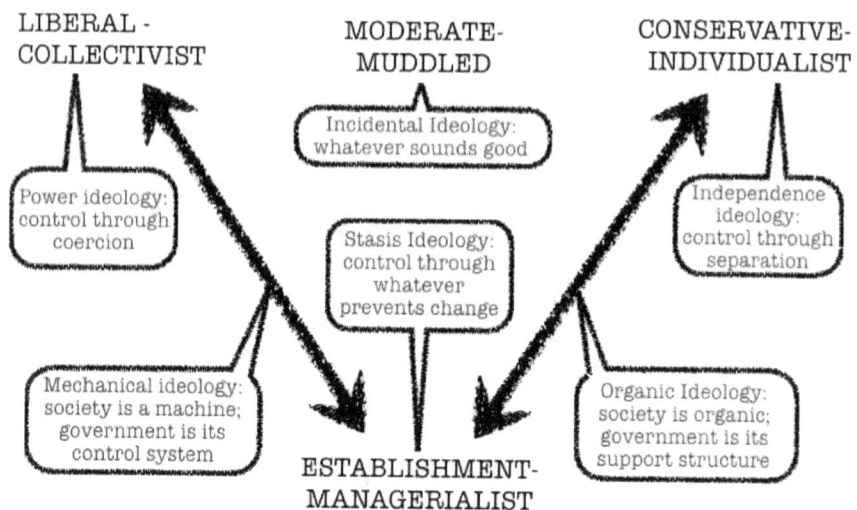

Improved Mental Model with nomenclature reflecting reality

Now that we have the geometry modeled correctly, let's look more closely at the labels, as shown in this figure. Words are the bricks in the architecture of ideas. We can no more construct a robust mental model from bad terminology than we could build a skyscraper from mud bricks. There is more to be said on this subject in the chapter, "On Communication", but for the moment, let's look at what we really mean when we use the words, "Liberal", "Establishment", "Moderate" & "Conservative".

☐ Liberal/Collectivist: The root of the word "coerce" is the Latin "arca" - a box. The goal of Liberalism is to collect people into

copyright © 2016 J. M. Payne

politically "correct" boxes. They do this by replacing the organic structures of society with the bureaucratic machinery of government. Their machine's purpose is to leave us with no other choice than to accept our place in the Collective's designated box.

☐ Establishment/Managerialist: These are the people who love the machinery of government for its own sake. Their priority is to protect their positions & privileges. They have no particular vision for the policies of the machine, as long as they're the ones in the driver's seat.

☐ Moderate/Muddled: They don't know much about the machinery or purpose of government. This is no accusation; it is simply a fact that, for any particular subject, most people do not spend a lot of effort thinking about it. Politics is no exception, & the result is that there are a considerable number of people whose politics is a muddle of opinions, not a coherent vision.

☐ Conservative/Individualist: The root of the word "constitute" is Latin for "that which was set up." Individualism is illustrated by C. S. Lewis' observation that "There are no ordinary people. You have never talked to a mere mortal. Nations, cultures, arts, civilizations - these are mortal, and their life is to ours as the life of a gnat. But it is immortals whom we joke with, work with, marry, snub and exploit - immortal horrors or everlasting splendors." So Conservatives approach politics with a vision that government is a temporary structure set up to support & protect individuals, not own & dominate them. Our Constitution is a blueprint for such a structure.

Now, every mental model is necessarily a simplification. Categories are a necessary simplification for any mental model. No particular person's thinking will fit any the above categories completely. The extreme corners in the diagram involve seeking control in different & dysfunctional ways. Collectivists (Liberals/Progressives), through coercion; Conservatives, through isolation; the Establishment, through stasis. Moderates prefer to assume that control is someone else's problem. There is no happy home in this picture, because politics is of this world & this world is not our home. Political, social & technical systems are merely vehicles to help us on our journey; they cannot be destinations. For any vehicle to work well, it must be balanced. A ship overloaded on one side will likely capsize; a airplane with one wing made of aluminum & the other of cast iron will crash, not fly. I am convinced that the organic strategy, where society is treated as a living thing that government is tasked to protect, is the best vehicle, & the Constitutional Conservative position provides the best balance for it. Yet any observer of recent history knows that this position, & Liberty

copyright 2016 © J. M. Payne

itself, have lost a lot of ground in America during the 20th century. We'll look next at why.

THE COERCIVE ALLIANCE

Liberty's retreat is due to the alliance between those who seek control as a means to an end & those who seek power as an end unto itself

Liberty has been in a protracted retreat in America because Collectivists & the Establishment have been cooperating from their love of & need for bigger government. We can call this the Coercive Alliance, since both factions advance their agendas through coercion. While this is quite discouraging, we must realize that it will not last, because while they work towards a common goal, they are driven by different values. The strain will build between them as they gather power. Collectivists will long to use that power to fundamentally transform society, while the Establishment will be jealously cling to that power as their indispensable prerogative. If ever they should succeed in achieving complete social domination (God forbid!), the rupture between them will be ugly & bloody., for the revolution always eats its children.

In the meantime, those of us who love liberty fight two enemies: Collectivists, who hate what we stand for, & the Establishment, which hates that we stand at all. We must take heart, because earlier generations stood against worse. America outlasted the nuclear threat of the USSR. It took on Nazi Germany & Imperial Japan at once &

copyright © 2016 J. M. Payne

> **Those who love liberty fight two enemies: Collectivists, who hate what we stand for, & the Establishment, which hates that we stand at all.**

defeated both. Abraham Lincoln fought the Confederate States & during the war won reelection running against one of his own Generals, George McClellan. In the American Revolution, Patriots had to contend with not only the British & their Hessians, but also the American Tories who sided with them. If we allow our freedom to be lost now, what can we say to the patriots who've gone before us? We would have to say, "You Continentals who marched barefoot in the snow, leaving a trail of bloody footprints; you Union soldiers who fought for four bloody years so a government of the people, by the people, for the people would not perish from the earth; you Allies who defeated the Axis powers in a war that spanned the world -- we're sorry, we lost the Liberty that was your legacy to us, to a bunch of smooth-talking politicians, without a shot being fired."

POLITICAL PARTY DYNAMICS

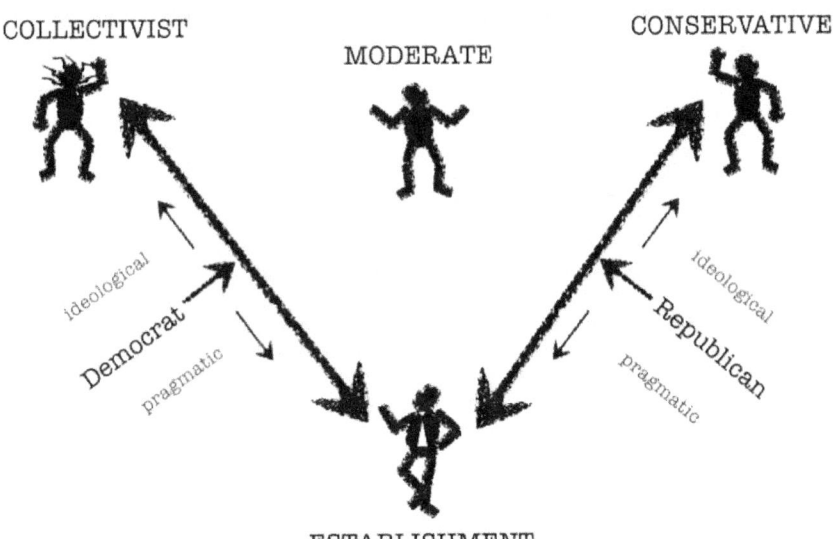

An effective political party is a team of opposites.

I have not mentioned political parties thus far (which may seem curious) because I conceive that political parties are the result of political dynamics, not their cause. Understanding the parties without understanding the underlying forces is like trying to understand how an

copyright 2016 © J. M. Payne

airplane flies without understanding aerodynamics. To be effective, a political party must combine both pragmatic & ideological elements. It must be able to take a stand & know when to cut a deal. When its party is in power, the pragmatic wing has the advantage; the agenda can be advanced by dispensing & withholding patronage. When out of power, the ideological wing must take the lead; the agenda must be advanced with persuasion & enthusiasm. If the idealists become dominant, the party will tend to devolve into a powerless mutual admiration society. If the pragmatists take over, the party will tend to become a soulless dealmaker, unable to lead in the crisis that tries the soul. It is the pragmatic-oriented, Establishment-leaning wings of the two major Parties that give rise to the complaint, "There's no difference between them!" But there is a real difference between the Parties' ideological wings; they operate from completely different mental models. The Collectivists & the Establishment tend operate from what I call the Mechanical Model; the Conservatives, from what I term the Organic Model. How a system operates follows from its structure, & its structure derives from the mental models of its creators. So, to change the results we must change the system & to change the system, we must change our mental models. The reason that our social problems have been impervious to political repair for the last few generations is not due to a lack of effort, intelligence, time, & certainly not money. I apprehend that it is because the mental model used conceiving & carrying out these efforts - the Mechanical Model - is fundamentally flawed.

copyright © 2016 J. M. Payne

The Mechanical Model

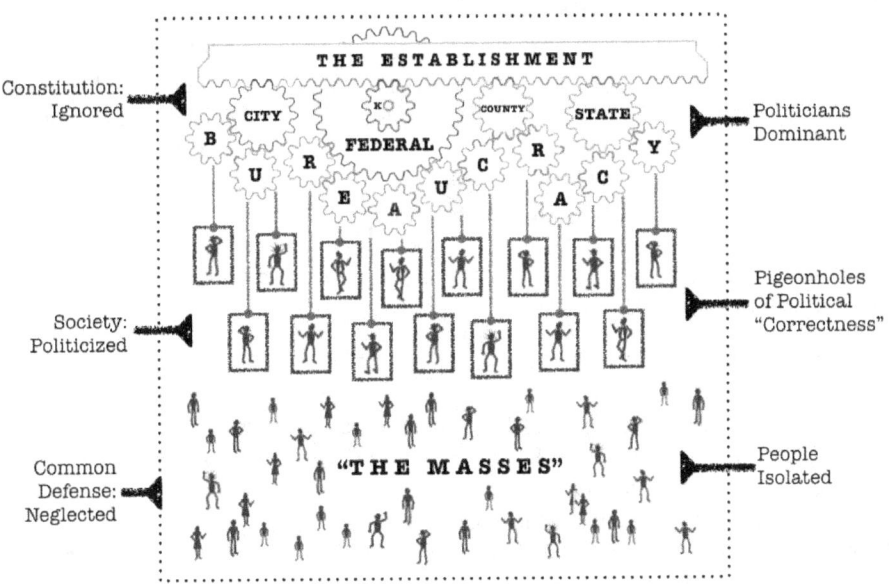

Motto: "If it feels good do it"

This Mechanical Model is diagrammed in the figure above. The emotional mainspring of it is the idea, "If it feels good, do it", or more poetically, "Follow your heart", or defiantly, "No one will tell me what's supposed to be right!" This is the root cause of the incoherence of Collectivism discussed earlier -- the practical problem of power. If I live by rule, "Follow your heart", others will, too. The inevitably conflicting desires that result can only be resolved by who has more power, not by who is right, because we abandoned the idea of the right & wrong when we chose to follow our hearts. Liberation from having to do the right thing is exactly what Collectivists seek, & political power is needed to achieve it. So, politicians, meshed with the Establishment & bureaucracy, form a powerful machine perched on top of society. As any observer of politics has seen, the rack & gears of this machine bind & clash; instead of being too big to fail, it is too big to succeed. Dangling

> **The mainspring of the Mechanical Model ... "No one will tell me what's supposed to be right!"**

from this mechanism are the pigeonholes of political "correctness". A variable alchemy of racial, economic, sexual, political & social factors determines the correct position of each pigeonhole. Below those privileged to be assigned a pigeonhole, are the Masses; helpless

copyright 2016 © J. M. Payne

individuals, cowering in the machine's shadow, hoping for a political change to their miserable state.

A constitution does not fit into this model. American Collectivists speak of a Living Constitution so that they may treat it as a dead letter & do what they like with political power. Laws then, exist mainly to empower the Better Sort of People, not to constrain power to protect the people's rights. Disturbingly, we hear people say, "We elect the President to run the country!" A king runs his country; a President serves his country. In criticizing the concentration of power in a throne, Thomas Paine, in Common Sense, relied on the Biblical account of the people of Israel asking the prophet Samuel for a king:

"This shall be the manner of the king that shall reign over you; ... he will appoint him captains ... & to make his instruments of war ... & he will take your daughters to be confectionaries & to be cooks & to be bakers (this describes the expense & luxury as well as the oppression of kings) & he will take your fields & your olive yards, even the best of them, & give them to his servants; & he will take the tenth ... of your vineyards, & give them to his officers & to his servants (by which we see that bribery, corruption, & favoritism are the standing vices of kings) & he will take the tenth of ... your goodliest young men ... & put them to his work; ... Nevertheless the People refused to obey the voice of Samuel, & they said, Nay, but we will have a king over us, that we may be like all the nations, & that our king may judge us, & go out before us & fight our battles."

> **Life is hard, then we die. If that is all there is, it is not enough to keep society going.**

As it was in ancient times, it was in Colonial times, & so it is now. As the Congress sinks into irrelevance, the Presidency becomes a throne. People come to, as Samuel Adams put it, "prefer the tranquility of servitude to the animating contest of freedom." And there are always politicians willing provide servitude for those who prefer it. If we imagine that such arrogance is bygone, consider the words of our current President, upon accepting his Party's nomination: "... this was the moment when the rise of the oceans began to slow & our planet began to heal ...". These are the words of one who sees government as a god. This is the idolatry in modern America. Because we have created our own god, there is "no fear of God before their eyes" for those operating from the Mechanical Model. It is based instead on fear of government, as described by John Adams, in "Thoughts on Government": "Fear is the foundation of most governments; but it is so sordid and brutal a passion, & renders men in whose breasts it predominates so stupid & miserable, that Americans will not be likely to

copyright © 2016 J. M. Payne

approve of any political institution which is founded on it." Not likely, unless after a long campaign of propaganda Americans are trained to fear government.

Paradoxically, a society operating on the Mechanical Model tends not to do well in providing for the common defense. Communist China could not win the Korean War, but they were viciously effective with Mao's Great Leap Forward. Nazi Germany diverted vital resources to continue their Holocaust, even as they were losing the war to the Allies. In America, Collectivist ambivalence on the common defense springs from their belief that what's wrong with the world is America. They are more interested in curing the world of American imperialism, colonialism, racism, & capitalism, than in defending the American people. This urge to "fix" America is why Collectivists want uncontrolled borders for the USA -- the low-wage illegal workers will become low-information voters for them. The ambivalence to foreign threats explains the cognitive dissonance of Collectivists regarding the military. In the face of the soldier, Collectivists see the truth of George Washington's declaration that, "Government is not reason, it ... is force", & this truth clashes unbearably with their vision of themselves as champions of compassion, fairness & reason.

> **... if we can't trust people to make their own decisions, then how can we trust politicians, who are people like us, to make decisions for everybody?**

The end state of this model is a society of three classes: the government machine on top, dependents on government under it & the masses on their own at the bottom. The model has an obvious flaw & a less apparent omission. The obvious flaw is making government the dominant structure of society. Government shall be the source from which all goodness flows, the temple at which all must bow. But this center cannot hold; it is too weak. The bare facts of human existence are dismal: life is hard, then we die. If that is all there is, it is not enough to keep society going.

The less apparent omission is family. People do not undertake the work & hazards of parenthood because of a cost-benefit calculation, or a bureaucratic mandate. Bringing children into this world is an act of outrageous cosmic optimism. Having a family is the hardest - & best - thing most of us ever do. As G. K. Chesterton put it, "The modern writers who have suggested...that the family is a bad institution, have generally confined themselves to suggesting...that perhaps the family is not always very congenial. Of course the family is a good institution because it is uncongenial .... It is, as the sentimentalists say, like a little kingdom, & like most other little kingdoms, is generally in a state of

copyright 2016 © J. M. Payne

something resembling anarchy." Yet, a society that fails in its families is a dead society walking. The unfolding demographic implosions in Western Europe, the former USSR, Japan & China offer sobering evidence of this truth. A full discussion of this dynamic is beyond this work, but see the documentaries, "Demographic Winter" & "Demographic Bomb" for an introduction. The real, but quiet catastrophe of demographic winter is far more dangerous to our future than the over-hyped threat of human-caused global warming, a modern superstition invented to justify control of our carbon emissions, thus controlling our energy & therefore, controlling us.

In a society so dominated by government, why bother with the risk & pain of creating an invention, or building a business? Better & easier to leave these important things to the Better Sort of people, who will dispense patronage & protection as they see fit, anyway. Society's natural communities wither because the artificial structure of government is used to overwrite society's organic systems. This is the fatal contradiction in the Mechanical Model: if we can't trust people to make their own decisions, then how can we trust politicians, who are people like us, to make decisions for everybody? What if the Better Sort of People are not actually <u>better</u>? Experience shows they are not. This is the system under which we have been laboring & losing ground. But there is a better, a tried & true way.

The Organic Model

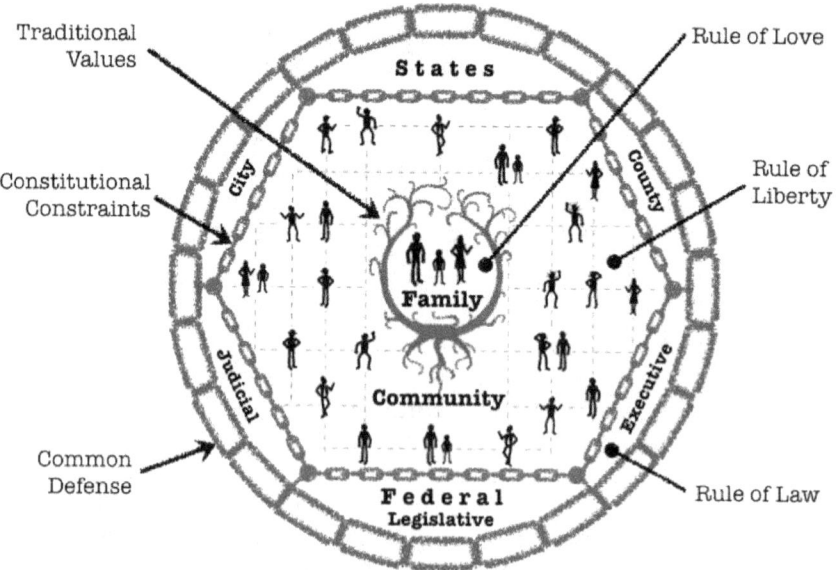

Motto: "Do the right thing"

copyright © 2016 J. M. Payne

We call this way the Organic Model, sketched above. It is built on the conviction that doing the right thing is what makes society work. The goodness that comes from this is what Conservatives seek to conserve. As Thomas Paine put it, society "produces happiness positively by uniting our affections", while government does so "negatively by restraining our vices". In this model, the government is constrained by a constitution to the system's periphery. Like a wall, it is positioned for our common defense.   Within that boundary, society has space for domestic tranquility where we can enjoy life, liberty & pursue happiness.   Constitutional limitations forbid government's intrusion into society's organic systems. This startling idea that power shall be restrained by words springs from America's Judeo-Christian roots. If the Almighty obliges Himself to be bound by covenants, how can mere politicians presume to exercise unlimited power? I don't presume to assign God a place in this model, though I do believe that it is aligned with the designs of that sublime Engineer. As a practical safeguard, powers are distributed among Local, State & Federal governments, with legislative, executive & judicial branches checking & balancing one another & our rights are recognized & protected in the Bill of Rights.

Now, one might say that architects design buildings, but in fact, architects design spaces. The entire purpose of a structure is the space that it creates. In the Organic Model, the purpose is not in the bricks & mortar of government – programs, laws, budgets & such. (Today, we've become so accustomed to laying government bricks, we didn't notice that we've bricked ourselves in.) The true purpose of government is to create the space in which community can breathe free & thrive. Community, not government, is where the goodness in society happens. When we live under the rule of liberty, we are not left "on our own" as Collectivists worry. We join freely into associations to fix our problems

> **"Government is not reason, it ... is force." -- George Washington**

& pursue our dreams.   In the 19th century, Alexis de Tocqueville described it this way: "In the United States associations are established to promote the public safety, commerce, industry, morality, & religion. There is no end which the human will despairs of attaining through the combined power of individuals united into a society." (Democracy in America, Book I, chapter 12.)

People organizing themselves under laws which they hold in common is true self-government. As John Adams put it on the eve of the American Revolution, in "Thoughts on Government": " ... there is no good government but what is republican...because the very definition of a republic is 'an empire of laws, and not of men'...best contrived to secure

copyright 2016 © J. M. Payne

an impartial and exact execution of the laws…" The idea of people making their own decisions under the rule of law is as old as Moses, who brought down from Mt. Sinai the 10 Commandments, not the 10 Bureaucracies. The Organic model requires a structural government. Structural government builds us a good road system; it doesn't control where & how we travel. It provides a stable, strong currency; it doesn't decide that Tom is more deserving than Dick & so Tom gets money from Harry's paycheck. It encourages hospitals & clinics; it doesn't put healthcare under a centralized command bureaucracy.   Structural government promotes education; it doesn't own & operate school systems. In the structural approach, freedom of religion means that politicians do not get to decide which beliefs are more legitimate; freedom of speech means they do not get to have an "off" switch for our microphones; freedom of the press means that they do not get to be our news editors; freedom of assembly means that we do not need our civic organizations to be licensed; redress of grievances means that politicians have to listen to our complaints. Indeed, granting politicians the power to "help" us with these rights is the surest way to lose them.

The Organic Model puts the family at the center. Families are the factories in which history is literally made. They are the bridges that transport our cultural DNA down through the generations. Creating a family is indeed an outrageous act of cosmic optimism, which people undertake because the very creation-fire of God burns within. In the Book of Genesis, the Creator did not begin by having Adam set up a government. Nor did He have Adam build a temple to start our story. He began our story with a family, by introducing Adam to Eve. She, not a priest nor a politician, was the Mother of us all. This is because the forces which must be invoked & contained to continue the human story are primordial & fierce. They can upend any government & knock down any temple. The family is the only viable containment vessel, operating under the rule of love, because only love can hold the center. For love to have room to work, power must constrained to certain parts of the system, but truth must be free to address all parts of the system; we

> **Creating a family is an outrageous act of cosmic optimism.**

must "speak the truth in love". So, religion -- which is how society sets the cornerstone of truth -- is not assigned a specific place in this model. Truth speaks to the government: "What does the Lord require of you, but to do justly, to love mercy, & to walk humbly with your God?" It speaks to the marketplace, "Be on your guard against all kinds of greed; a man's life does not consist in the abundance of his possessions." Truth speaks to the family, "The two will become one flesh....Therefore what God has joined together, man must not separate".

copyright © 2016 J. M. Payne

This conceptual blueprint - family firmly at the center, government fixed at the boundaries, & community free to flourish in between - has served America well since before its founding.   Engineering experience has taught me that 80% of a project's success is determined in the initial 20% of effort, the conceptual phase. Get the fundamental concept right, & problems tend to be manageable.   Get the fundamental concept wrong, difficulties are certain & disaster all too likely. Collectivism - the Mechanical society - is a fundamentally flawed concept.   It is based on fear: fear of failure, fear of being a victim, & above all, fear of government.   And as John Basil Barnhill said, "Where the people fear the government you have tyranny. Where the government fears the people you have liberty." So Collectivism is not a good idea that simply costs too much; it's a bad idea that costs too much.

Now that we've clarified our thinking, the task is to renovate the house that Liberty built. Any renovation requires both a good understanding of the flaws in the existing structure & a good plan for the renewed building. I've proposed that our society's problem is that it has been gradually transformed to fit the Mechanical Model. I submit that the renovation should restore the blueprint of the Organic Model.   If the function of a building is in the spaces it creates, then we can't change that with new paint on old walls, or new signs on old doors.   A more fundamental transformation is required. Let the results we want -- life, liberty & a chance for happiness -- determine the shape of the structure. But in order to change the structure, we have to communicate with each other, because in culture & politics, if you can't communicate, you don't exist.

copyright 2016 © J. M. Payne

III. On Communication

"The speech ... is nothing better than a willful & audacious libel against the truth, the common good ... offering up of human sacrifices to the pride of tyrants." – Thomas Paine, Common Sense, Appendix

"... eloquence may strike the ear, & the language of sorrow draw forth the tear of compassion, but nothing can reach the heart that is steeled with prejudice." – Thomas Paine, The Crisis No. 1

That the Collectivist approaches to government -- Liberalism, Progressivism, Socialism, Fascism or Communism -- produce social failure, is obvious to anyone who looks honestly at history. That Collectivists continue to be a political force is due to their great expertise in illusion, supported by a deep investment in communication. They use emotional imagery to sell their "if it feels good, do it" philosophy to our hearts through video media. Conservatism appeals to our heads & so Conservatives tend to be strong in audio & print media. Conservatives have the right ideas, but do not take the time to craft the right words, the right stories, & the right vision, to communicate them. This failure to communicate reduces Conservatives to arguing that Collectivism "sounds good, but..." & what follows the "but..." can easily be used to make Conservatives sound cold & harsh. What's lost in that scenario is opportunity to point out that Collectivism is an addiction to power.   Too much of Conservatives' internet, broadcast & print bandwidth is wasted on an ongoing amazement that those addicted to power act like any other kind of addict.   They will tell any lie, expend any resource, betray any trust, to get more of what they crave. This is not a negotiation with political opponents over policy.   It is in an intervention, with the stakes being not merely an individual's future, but the future of our whole society.

Conservatives' communication has been hobbled with an apologetic agenda, defined by fear of the opposition.   Perhaps this is because Conservatives, being inclined to mind their own business, are reluctant to push an aggressive agenda.   Yet, Collectivists don't constrain themselves in this way. They loudly, shamelessly proclaim their right to

> **We are not engaged in a negotiation with political opponents over policy. We are engaged in an intervention with politicians who are addicted to power**

run everyone's lives. If this delusion is not broken, then whether the Conservative agenda is apologetic or aggressive is irrelevant, because it will never be implemented. Let's agree that our priority is to break this addiction to power, cooperating when we can, & tolerating dissent

copyright © 2016 J. M. Payne

where we disagree. The Declaration of Independence's claim that "We hold these truths to be self-evident, that all men are created equal..." implies that all voices ought to be heard, & leads us directly to the 1st Amendment's protection of freedom of speech. So our duty is to participate, communicate, make contacts, get experience, work where we can, on whatever issues we choose, with whatever groups we can find or create.

Ronald Reagan was a great communicator & one of the things that made him great was that he smiled so much more than he frowned. So, whenever we communicate, with opposition or allies, we should always try to find something for which we can say "Thank you!" Practically everyone that an elected official meets, wants something -- either for the official to do something, or to feel ashamed for something he already did, or did not, do. It is exhausting, & a major reason why so few good citizens run for office, leaving the field to those who simply crave power. A spoonful of sugar helps the medicine go down, so don't forget the sugar. Reagan also was a great Conservative, but he was only one man. He was not able to turn the whole society around. That kind of change requires the whole ethos of society be reformed. No singular leader or

> **So we eat the pig ...The more of us doing the eating, the faster the pig gets eaten.**

small group of heroes can do that. Therefore, I apprehend that we must no longer pursue a Big Fish Strategy: find a big fish, with big teeth & a big bite, to speak for our values & against our opponent's. I propose instead a Piranha Strategy: millions of fish, tens of millions of teeth, & billions of bites. That's how the little piranhas eat the big pig. And Collectivism is a big pig, like the one in Orwell's "Animal Farm" that solemnly declared, "some animals are _more_ equal than others". That pig has waded into our water & is fouling it. So we eat the pig. Some of us can bite into the parts of the pig labeled "financial insanity"; others, the parts called "social catastrophe". The more of us doing the eating, the faster the pig gets eaten. In terms of communication, we have three rows of teeth to use: stories, questions, & words. The 1st row of teeth are the stories we tell.

STORIES: Jesus of Nazareth had no armies, no wealth, wrote no books, & built no great organizations during His time on earth. Yet He changed the world with His words. Many of those words were given in the form of stories. The Gospels contain some 46 parables. These stories have penetrated & shaped our culture far beyond the reach of religion -- the stories of the good Samaritan & the prodigal son, for example. Each of His stories was short, pointed & accessible to His audience. If we want

copyright 2016 © J. M. Payne

to be effective beyond the limited scope of political power, then we should imitate His tactics.

To offer an small example: "Suppose my neighbor pulled up in his driveway in a brand-new car, & I went over to admire it. He asks if I could help him unload his new car, which is packed with new stuff. As he grabs one end of a 60 inch TV & I grab the other, I quip, 'Somebody must have gotten a big promotion!' 'No', he replies, 'actually, I just got laid off.' I nearly drop my end of the TV. He continues, 'I figured I better charge all of this on credit now, because as soon as the they find out I'm out of work, my credit will be no good.' I almost call my neighbor an idiot, but then I realize that he has simply done with his situation what Washington politicians have done with our country's economy."

And here is another: "There was once a strong, young lumberjack who was convinced that it was time for the senior lumberjack in his community to step aside. So he challenged him to a woodchopping contest. The young lumberjack began with confidence, & it seemed justified, as the younger man pulled ahead. Then, the older man stopped working & took a break! The young buck thought, 'This will be easier than I thought!' But the old man wasn't done; he soon resumed his steady pace. As the day wore on, the old man closed the gap. So, the young man swung his axe even faster. Yet, the old man slowly gained; & incredibly, he kept taking breaks. At day's end, despite the increasingly desperate efforts of the younger man, the old lumberjack had won. Amazed & ashamed, the loser asked him, 'How did you do it? I know I worked harder than you & you even stopped to rest!' The old lumberjack looked hard at his rival, then reached into his pocket & pulled out his whetstone. 'Boy,' he said, 'I wasn't just catching my breath on those breaks -- I was sharpening my axe.'"

> **We are not merely arguing with political opponents, but are wrestling with hearts darkened by a beautiful lie.**

This 2nd story also illustrates how we need to approach stories. Simply writing, "sharpening your axe is a good idea", would be quickly forgotten. But putting it in a story makes the point stick. Stories touch the heart, not just the head. If we are to change the disastrous course that we are on, we must engage both the hearts & minds of our fellow citizens. We are not merely arguing with political opponents, but are wrestling with hearts darkened by a beautiful lie. So, let's expand on this little story with the Lumberjack Rules for Communication:

Sharpen your blade. A sharp axe is a safe ax, & gets the job done faster. Now, sensible people gather the facts, analyze options & then form conclusions. Conservatives, being sensible, prefer this approach. But

copyright © 2016 J. M. Payne

there is not time for this process on TV, on radio, or in political communication generally. We must hone our arguments ahead of time, make them sharp enough to fit into a sound bite or onto a bumper sticker. We must distill our message, as if being charged $100 per word, down to concise phrases that cut through the noise. To develop this skill, make a practice of saving selections of your internet comments, social media postings, emails, letters to the editor & to elected officials, etc., in a file which you then organize, edit, & sharpen your message. Then cut & paste from it as needed.

Start early. Haste while using an ax is a good way to end up in the emergency room. Better to start early & work steadily. Getting an early start is indispensable in communication, because the 1st commenters set the terms of the discussion. Timeliness in communication is supported by the rule of sharpening the axe, of having the message ready to go. The Minutemen of the Colonial era were ready to exchange gunfire at a moment's notice; can't we be ready to exchange words as quickly?

Lead with the sharp edge. An axe works by putting the weight of the head behind the sharp edge. This is the reverse of the Conservative inclination to build a case step-by-step to end with a sound conclusion. But, lack of time & short attention spans mean we can't "leave the best 'til last." We have to put the sharp conclusion out there 1st. If time allows elaboration, do so; if not, then the key question or idea has been planted in the people's minds. (And it is the larger audience, not the immediate opponent, who is the real target.) Ideas open the mind like a plow opens the soil; then the truth can take root. With time, its growth can undermine even entrenched bigotry & incoherence.

Cut to the root. To cut down a tree, you don't trim the branches until the tree is gone; you swing the ax at the base of the trunk, the root of the problem. Arguing the details of a proposed increase in political control means surrendering the question of whether that control should exist at all. The issue is, which takes priority: the collective need for control or individual human rights? When Collectivists object, "But people will make the wrong choice!" they are slandering the rest of us as being too foolish to be trusted. The root error here is the hidden implication that Collectivists must be trusted to choose for us all. So, we attack that idea, not just this particular application of it. Cutting to the root also means not cutting at the opponent. Most people arguing the side of Collectivism are sincerely wrong. Even if your opponent is completely mercenary, what good does it do to say so? You say they're bad, they say you're bad, & the issue gets lost in the name-calling. Personal destruction is a favorite Alinskyite tactic & gives the advantage to our opponents. Anger hardens hearts; grace softens them.

copyright 2016 © J. M. Payne

"Let your conversation be gracious & effective so that you will have the right answer for everyone".

As an example, instead of talking heads presenting charts, tables & warnings about the massive Federal debt, why not make a video showing small children on a playground, struggling because each has a huge, heavy duffle bag strapped & locked to their backs, labeled, "$19

> **Words are the weapons in the battle of ideas; so why let our opponents choose our weapons for us?**

TRILLION DEBT"?   The narrator would be saying, in a concerned, motherly voice, "Why are we letting the politicians do this to our children? ... Is big government worth the price they will have to pay? ... Let's set our children free from the greed of the political class ..." This aims at the heart; after the heart is moved, then the mind can be changed with facts & figures.

When Collectivists say, "Justice for the poor demands that the minimum wage be at least $15 an hour!", our typical response is a lecture: "Well, you are not properly accounting for the macro- & micro-economic effects of marginal wage increases on entry-level employment...blah, blah, blah...", & everyone's eyes glaze over.   I propose that a more effective response would be, "We can't trust politicians to set anybody's wages -- we don't even trust them to set their own!   Where do you get the idea that politicians are saints, but the rest of us are selfish?" This is concise, it cuts to the heart of the matter -- trusting politicians -- & it corrects the question from, "What should wages be?" to "Who should set wages?".   It does not attack the immediate opponent as being stupid or deceptive, but casts doubt on idea of trusting those in power. And one of the most powerful ways to cast doubt on a lie is to ask good questions. So, the next row of teeth we have are questions.

QUESTIONS: The armor-piercing rounds in our arsenal are penetrating questions that punch through the layers of emotional pseudo-thought, rattle the target's mental models & force real thinking to begin.   Some examples for consideration:

☐ We make fun of government defense procurement -- $600 hammers & $1000 toilet seats -- so why is it a good idea to force everyone to get healthcare through government procurement?

☐ If we don't trust politicians, why do we give them so much power over our health care, schools, jobs & money?

copyright © 2016 J. M. Payne

☐ If the 1st Amendment prohibits politicians from controlling what's preached in the churches, & what's reported by the press, why do we let them control what's taught in the schools?

☐ How can we have social justice when we allow any category of people to be defined as subhuman & disposed of at will, through abortion?

☐ Should a "mixed-race" adopted child benefit from, or be punished by, so-called Affirmative Action programs? What about a recent immigrant who has dark skin, but comes from privileged circumstances?

☐ If it's wrong to treat women as sex objects, why is it right for the pornography industry to profit from treating women as sex objects?

☐ Why don't those who preach tolerance practice tolerance by leaving the Christmas Tree & Nativity scene in the town square alone?

☐ Why is it greed when a corporation raises the price of its products, but not when politicians raise the price (taxes) of their product (government)?

☐ With all the problems teachers have to deal with -- gang violence, teen pregnancy, single parent families, illiteracy -- do teachers, at the end of the day, wish "Oh, if only politicians would give us standards to teach to (like Common Core)"?

☐ If government is supposed to stay out of our bedrooms, why is government forcing us to embrace gay marriage?

☐ We insist that we can prevent kids from using tobacco, but when it comes to sex, we can't control what kids do?

☐ About 10 times as many people die because of cars than guns. Cars aren't protected by a Constitutional Amendment. So, if it's all about saving lives, where's the campaign to ban cars?

☐ Politicians say "spreading the wealth" is good for society; but what they actually do is take from the productive to buy themselves reelection -- isn't that really just "passing the loot"?

☐ If we're supposed to trust politicians, then couldn't the Constitution just say, "We, the People, trust you, the politicians"?

The final row of teeth we have, the smallest & yet the sharpest, are the words we use to craft our stories & frame our questions.

WORDS: Words are the weapons in the battle of ideas; so why let our opponents choose our weapons for us? They are more than mere weapons -- they define the terrain of the battlefield, the high ground &

copyright 2016 © J. M. Payne

the killing ground. Letting our opponents control our lexicon is like surrendering the high ground before the battle even starts. We must boldly choose words grounded in truth instead of accepting words that support the Collectivist lie: that they are the Better Sort of People, entitled to control us all for our own good. I offer the following then, as a starting point for our Lexicon for Liberty. Develop the habit of mind to question accepted terms & refuse to use them, & to find true words & use them instead.

A LEXICON for LIBERTY		
COLLECTIVIST	CONSERVATIVE	COMMENTS
abortion, choice	baby-killing, infanticide	A euphemism is often just a lie trying to be respectable.
activist	agitator	"Activist" sounds positive; agitators are divisive.
affirmative action	political patronage	A highly distilled euphemism vs. the reality of the Establishment's power.
anti-discrimination laws	political preferencing laws	The Establishment deciding what groups will be privileged & which punished.
big business	big producers	The Establishment protects its fiefdoms; Liberty rewards creation & production.
big government	fat government	No explanation needed, really.
bringing home the bacon	passing out the loot	Politicians buying the votes of the majority by looting the the productive.
capitalism	economic freedom	"Capitalism" sounds like "decapitation" & "capital punishment" & leaves out "freedom".
closed primary	fair primary	Republicans choosing their candidate & Democrats choosing theirs is fair.
Common Core Standards	Crony Capitalist Standards	It's about selling curriculum, not teaching children.
comprehensive reform	special interest accommodation	"Comprehensive" is Establishment-speak for "special interests are on board".
cuts (regulatory, spending, taxes)	relief, restraint (regulatory, spending, taxes)	"Cuts" hurt, bleed & need stitches; "relief" is always welcome; to "restraint" is protection.
Democratic Party	Plantation Party	Founded on the slave plantation & never gave up the dream of being our masters.

copyright © 2016 J. M. Payne

A LEXICON for LIBERTY		
COLLECTIVIST	CONSERVATIVE	COMMENTS
deregulation	liberation	"De-" is negative; "liberate" is positive.
entitlement program	dependency program	People in these programs aren't gaining ownership; they are being owned by the Establishment.
family values	value families	"Family values" can mean anything; "value families" means putting family above other interests.
feminist	androgynist	We are not interchangeable biological units of production (with only minor plumbing differences).
fetus	baby	"Fetus" is medical; a "baby" is human.
gay marriage	androgynous marriage	We are not interchangeable biological units of production (with only minor plumbing differences).
gun ban	gun monopoly	The real goal of "banning" guns to give the Establishment a monopoly on them.
gun-free zone	free-fire zone, unarmed victim zone	Because a "no guns allowed" sign only stops people who obey the rules.
gun rights	human right of self-defense	Things don't have rights; people do; self-defense is a fundamental human right.
hate crime laws	political crime laws	Let the punishment fit the crime, not the politics of the criminal.
illegal immigrant	exploitable immigrant	The Establishment imports illegals to get low-wage labor & low-information voters.
income tax	productivity tax	Income doesn't just happen by accident - it must be produced.
Independent Payment Advisory Board (IPAB)	Death Panel	Anytime the Establishment sets up "independent" boards, they are dodging accountability.
Internal Revenue Service (IRS)	Federal Tax Agency	Anytime the Establishment names something with euphemisms, beware.
limited government	structural government	"Limited" implies that our government is just too much of a good thing; "structural" implies strength without activism.

copyright 2016 © J. M. Payne

A LEXICON for LIBERTY		
COLLECTIVIST	**CONSERVATIVE**	**COMMENTS**
living Constitution	dead-letter Constitution	If the Constitution means whatever politicians want, then it's a dead letter.
mainstream journalist	establishment journalist	Journalism is about getting the story, not parroting the Establishment's line.
marriage equality	marriage erased	Because if marriage can mean anything, then it means nothing.
minimum wage	political wage	We can't trust the politicians to set our wages.
moderate voter	muddled voter	Because they're not thinking things through.
multiculturalism	anti-Americanism	American culture is what is being displaced.
negative rights	protected rights	"Negative rights" are political powers denied to the government.
no-fault divorce	no-fairness divorce	Because the bad actor in the marriage gets off without accountability.
ObamaCare	ObamaControl	Putting politicians between sick people & doctors is about control, not care.
open primary	false primary	Non-members choosing the Parties' candidates is false, not fair.
original intent of the Constitution	structure of the Constitution	"Original" sounds out-of-date; "intent" is slippery; but "structure" implies function.
Patient Centered Outcomes Research Institute (PCORI)	Death Panel	Anytime the Establishment uses euphemisms & sets up "independent" groups, we should be very afraid.
Patient Protection & Affordable Care Act	Political Patronage & Unaffordable Control Act	A euphemism is often just a lie trying to be respectable.
pork barrel spending	pass the loot spending	Elected officials buy the votes of the majority by looting the productive.
positive rights	political privileges	"Positive rights" are indistinguishable from political powers.
price controls	political pricing	We can't trust the Establishment to set prices for the things we need.

copyright © 2016 J. M. Payne

A LEXICON for LIBERTY		
COLLECTIVIST	CONSERVATIVE	COMMENTS
private (economy, sector, enterprise)	productive (economy, sector, enterprise)	"Private" sounds like a backyard hobby; in fact, productivity is the backbone of our economy.
privatization	liberation	When control is taken away from the government, it is liberated, not privatized.
progressive taxes	oppressive taxes	When we start to move up financially, "progressive" taxes press us back down.
public (economy, enterprise, investment, sector,)	political (economy, enterprise, investment, sector,)	"Public" implies the government is selflessly seeking the general welfare, not serving its own political interests.
public (school, education)	government (school, education)	"Public" implies the government selflessly serving children, not propagandizing our children for its interests.
public-private partnership	cronyism	The Establishment is the senior partner, special interests are junior partners, & the rest of us are the "paying partners".
revenue enhancement	added tax burden, political greed, political profiteering	"Enhancement" & "revenue" both sound good, but really it's just politicians increasing the price of government.
sexual revolution	sexual devolution	We've devolved life's creation into mere recreation.
single payer health care	single chooser health care	That single chooser will be the government.
social engineering	political manipulation	Society is organic; it should be nurtured, not manipulated.
social justice	political preference	"Social justice" is the government giving out preferences; it is neither social, nor justice.
social program	dependency program	There's nothing social about being dependent on the government.
Social Security	Senior Dependency	"Social Security" made retirement dependent on politicians.
Socialism	Collectivism	There is nothing "social" in replacing society's organic systems with collective control machinery.

copyright 2016 © J. M. Payne

A LEXICON for LIBERTY		
COLLECTIVIST	CONSERVATIVE	COMMENTS
socialized (medicine, health care)	politicized (medicine, health care)	When medicine is taken over by the government, it is politicized, not socialized.
spread the wealth	pass the loot	Politicians buy the votes of the majority by looting the productive.
sustainable development	sustainable control	Because that's what the Establishment is seeking to sustain -- their control.
tax cut	tax relief	"Cuts" hurt & bleed; "relief" reduces the burden that the Establishment puts on the people.
tax expenditure tax spending	tax favoritism	"Expenditure" & "spending" imply that everything belongs to the government; "favoritism" is government playing favorites with the tax code.
undocumented workers	exploitable workers	The Establishment imports illegals to get low-wage labor & low-information voters.
universal health care	politicized medical control	It's not "universal", nor "healthy", nor "caring".
War on Terror	War Against Islamofascism	We cannot successfully fight what we will not honestly name.
War on Women	War Against the Family	Because the family is what stops the Establishment from politicizing everything.
welfare program	dependency program	People in these aren't "faring well", but becoming dependent on the government.
working families	American families	Because the purpose of families is not to produce workers for the Establishment.

This list is offered to help us disrupt Collectivist propaganda & communicate our message better. But it is all for nothing if we fail to take the last step -- closing the deal. All too often we hear or read Conservatives in full-bore outrage saying, "Look at what Liberals are doing! How can they get away with doing that!" But we fail to tie Collectivists' bad behavior back to their fundamentally bad idea: that we need to give them power to make the important decisions for us. We don't call for a rejection of Collectivism in its entirety. We are defeated in detail, because we fail to tie the problem at hand to the big picture, & then ask for the big change.

copyright © 2016 J. M. Payne

Consider the human right of self-defense, protected by the Constitution's 2nd Amendment. How many words are wasted arguing over magazine capacities & what type of guns hunters really need, instead of the primary question: can we trust politicians to have a monopoly on firearms? Instead of losing our audience in long, technical arguments, we should use an honest vocabulary to ask good, hard questions & to tell stories that go to the heart of the matter.

Collectivism is an addiction to power; history shows it to be as addictive as any drug. Addicts sometimes claim to work & think better when using their drug. Addiction produces a false but powerful faith, which can work for a time. In a similar way, the Democratic Party, the political home of Collectivism, has been winning because of the faith they have in the power of power. Now, Collectivism is a lie & does not work. But they believe -- so they fight, & so they win. There have been

> **Do we believe in God & Liberty more than our opposition believes in Government & Collectivism? That is the question.**

Republicans who knew how to believe & fight & win. Abraham Lincoln & the founding Republicans did not try to cut a deal for a kinder, gentler sort of slavery. They were determined to end slavery, because they knew slavery is evil. Ronald Reagan did not go to the Brandenburg Gate to cut a deal with Mr. Gorbachev so that we could live with the Berlin Wall. He went over there & said, "Mr. Gorbachev, tear down this wall!", because he knew the Soviet empire was evil. These Republicans believed in something -- they believed in Liberty. They fought for it & they won for it.

So, what will it be? Are we going to go on losing under the pastel banner of "electability"? Or are we going to lift up the banner of bold colors, & stand up for of the truth on which our nation was founded? The truth that there is no "Better Sort of People"; that people are created equal, gifted by our Creator with human rights -- to live, to be free, to seek happiness; & that government's purpose is to defend our people & secure our rights, with means granted by our consent. Do we believe in God & Liberty more fiercely than the opposition believes in Government & Collectivism? That is the question. Who believes the most, will fight the hardest & will most likely win. When we find our faith, we will find our voice to call on people to reject that big lie & embrace the self-evident truth. And knowing the truth sets us free.

copyright 2016 © J. M. Payne

Top-Down vs. Bottom-Up

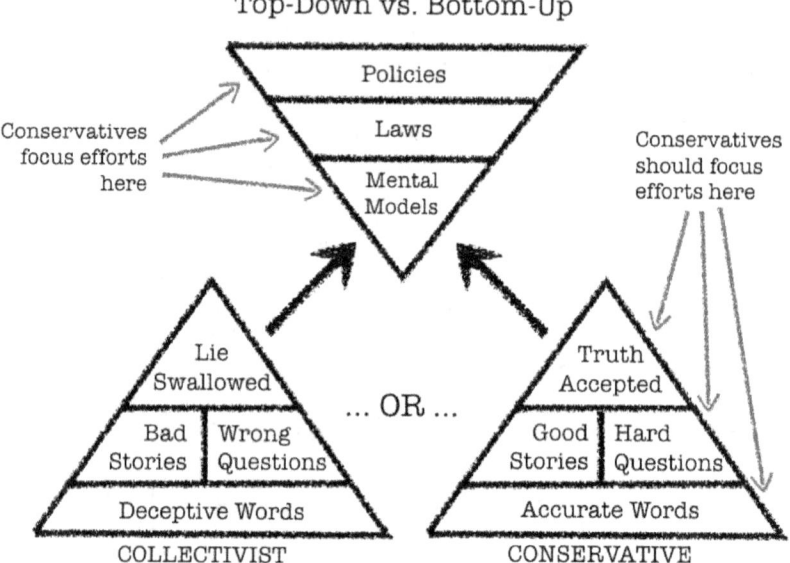

What's implemented in the top triangle depends on what's believed in the bottom one

If we are to fight, we must pick the battlefield strategically. This a battle that is not fought just at the level of policies, laws & procedures, but in the words, questions & stories that shape the thinking that inform them, as illustrated in the diagram. What society accepts as truth drives what government implements as law. The beauty & balance of our Constitution's articles & amendments spring from the truths in our Declaration of Independence. But those truths were only self-evident to the founding generation because they were steeped in narratives from the Bible, had grappled with the hard questions that an honest study of history raises, & had built their mental models with words that, for all their eloquence, were well grounded in reality. Today, our people have been taught deceptive definitions for the words with which we think. We ask the wrong questions about society & government, & so all too frequently accept lies for truths. Limiting ourselves to railing against Collectivists' dysfunctional policies, bad laws & warped doctrines, is like trying to repair a building built on a flawed foundation. No matter how hard we work to fix the doors, unstick the windows & patch the cracks, the problems keep coming back, because the foundation is not being addressed. As Jesus of Nazareth taught, we must be like "...a wise man who built his house on the rock & the rain descended, the floods came, & the winds blew & beat on that house; & it did not fall, for it was founded on the rock." For too long we have been like "... a foolish man who built his house on the sand & the rain descended, the floods came, & the

copyright © 2016 J. M. Payne

winds blew and beat on that house; & it fell. And great was its fall." The storm is upon us, & there is little time left.

copyright 2016 © J. M. Payne

IV. On a Structure for Liberty

"In the following pages, I offer nothing more than simple facts, plain arguments, & common sense" -
Thomas Paine, Common Sense, Chapter III

The essence of Liberty is improvisation. But our freedom to improvise, innovate, adapt & overcome, has been hobbled by the Collectivist agenda of a "better" society through bigger government.   For the century past, the two political parties have been defined by that agenda. Democrats were enthusiastically for it, Republicans reluctantly accepted it.   Whenever a 3rd party arose, if its concerns could be correlated to that agenda, they would be co-opted by one of the main parties. If not, that 3rd party would end up essentially talking to itself. This result is not due to some vast conspiracy. It is inherent in our national political structure. The Framers of our Constitution wisely designed this structure so that fundamental transformation can happen only by the agreement of a large majority, over an extended time. The 1st prize in this system is to set the agenda; 2nd prize is being able to veto parts of that agenda; 3rd prize is, "Have a nice trip home." In such a system, the increasing centralization of power that we've seen predictably produces the political polarization that everyone hates, for the higher the stakes are, the more vicious the struggle will be.

While this stable, dialectic structure is well suited to politics, it is completely inadequate for the rest of society. The assumption that large institutions & individuals can coexist without independent mediating institutions is one of the deep conceptual flaws of Collectivist ideology. The "social engineers" (as a real engineer, I find this term to be offensive) presume that society's vital functions can be hammered into submission by centralized bureaucracies. If the government's tool is a hammer, then every problem seems like a nail. And, if the problem isn't a nail, hammer it anyway.   For example, we've stubbornly held for decades to the idea that children's education is just a public utility, like electricity or sewers. In fact, the structure of human society flows from human nature. It cannot be engineered for the needs of bureaucracy nor configured to the latest political fashion. The mediocrity & misery that has plagued government-centric societies resulted from their denial of human nature.   The flaw is in the design, not the implementation.

The flaw in us, that Collectivists claim to want to fix, is greed. Whether greed is good is not the question. The fact is, greed is real; the question is, "How best to deal with it?" Collectivists see coercion as the solution; government will force the rest of us to restrain our greed. But what will restrain the Collectivists' greed? In contrast, Conservatives see liberty

copyright © 2016 J. M. Payne

as the solution; competition will make greed work against itself. This requires clear, simple laws, that are enforced fairly; laws that respect people's rights & liberties, instead of granting politicians the power to decide who succeeds & fails. This would be a complete reversal in the direction our politics has been heading for the last century. Instead of politicians fundamentally transforming our society, the people will have to fundamentally transform politics. But how can we hope to make this change?

First, we admit the reality of the addiction. The Establishment & Moderates are like the family members who stubbornly refuse to believe that dear, old Uncle Sam is an addict: "He promised that, this time, really & truly, he'll bring his spending under control, if we'll just lend him a couple of Trillion dollars more..." We must 1st agree that Uncle Sam is an addict, then separate him from the focus of his addiction. For an alcoholic, we'd get rid of all alcohol in the house; for a gambler, we'd cut off his access to money, credit & the internet. For Collectivists, we have to separate them from political power. Discredit their ideas, defeat them in elections, defund their organizations, deprive them of cover in the judicial system. Then we constitute a structure of government that doesn't enable their addiction. Shrink the political economy & grow the

> **"He promised that, this time, really & truly, he'll bring the spending under control, if we'll just lend him a couple of Trillion dollars more..."**

productive economy. Consolidate, eliminate & reduce in scope & funding all dependency & regulatory programs. Restore the vertical separation of powers. Establish freedom of education. Provide automatic sunsetting of all laws & regulations. Slay that vile worm, the gerrymander. This road won't be easy or short, but it does lead to where we want to go. A place where schoolchildren are as astonished to learn that people once thought that politicians should decide who sees a doctor, as they are now to learn that people once thought that who eats at a lunch counter should be decided by skin color.

In the period between the Contract with America & President George W. Bush's reelection, there was hope that we were ready to face our addiction to power. All that was needed was leadership. Regrettably, there was none. The 1st milepost on this dead-end road was the failure to defend Speaker Newt Gingrich from the relentless attacks directed at him. The next was the abortive attempt to reform Social Security. The final one was the Bush-Kennedy Education Bill, the so-called No Child Left Behind law. Having lost the resolve to kick the addiction, Republicans then went on a spending binge worthy of the Democrats. Clearly they wanted merely to manage the vast control machine of

copyright 2016 © J. M. Payne

government, not dismantle it. This neither quenched the Collectivists' lust for more control, nor satisfied people's desire for real change. It was blood in the water for the Democrats. As Rush Limbaugh noted, even when they were the minority, Democrats acted as if they were the majority. The sad end of this halfhearted time on the wagon was the Republicans' sweeping defeats in 2006 & 2008.

More outrage at the increasing politicization of every aspect of America life will change nothing. Addicts do not reform because people get mad at them. Change happens when they realize that their addiction is killing them, & they choose life instead. We need hopeful evangelism for restoring our liberty as much as dire warnings against looming tyranny. The windows for such fundamental changes are neither large nor frequent. We cannot afford to let any more of them pass. There is hope rising from the grass-roots that we still have the will to turn back from destruction & work for renewal.

This renewal cannot merely be political; the problem is larger than politics. The changes must work across the all organs of society -- family, work, worship, finance, & government. The disease is systemic,

---

The disease is systemic, so the treatment must be comprehensive.

---

so its treatment must be comprehensive. We are all going to have to contribute to the solution. No one person or group can prescribe a neat, simple remedy. The ideas outlined below are mostly not original to me, but we are not assigning credit in an academic exercise. Take these as seeds for your thinking, as the full development of the changes needed are well beyond the scope of this small work:

☐ Family. The war against the family must end, because it undermines the foundation of our society. Laws to restore & protect this cornerstone of society must be passed & enforced. But even if all the laws were fixed today, our families would not be healthy tomorrow. The effect of "no-fault" (really, no-fairness) divorce has been the "no-success" marriage, with scars inflicted on the souls husbands, wives & children. Those hearts must be mended, & that will require grace, support, mercy & patience in churches, charities, schools & communities.

☐ Education. Many deceptive words, bad stories & wrong questions have taken root from the decades-long grip of Collectivism on schools. The National Education Association is not what its name implies. Instead it is a 2nd rate labor union & a 1st rate auxiliary of the Democratic Party. Schools liberated from government

copyright © 2016 J. M. Payne

monopoly, through homeschooling, localization, charters, vouchers, etc., will be needed to reweave education into family & community. Education as a lifelong discipline must replace the current scheme of school as a factory-style process.

☐ Heath care.   It's said that if we don't have out health we have nothing.   Then what do we have, when politicians control our healthcare?   We have nothing but what they decide to let us have. So why not:

- Transfer the health care tax break from employers to us so that it's portable instead of tied to our jobs;

- Create health insurance bonds so that people can buy insurance in advance & thereby prevent loss of coverage due to financial reversal or pre-existing conditions, yet without rewarding irresponsible behavior;

- Repeal the laws preventing interstate competition & variety in health insurance, because competition, not regulation, creates excellence;

- Allow health insurance to be priced by risk so that healthy behavior is rewarded & those who make unhealthy choices take responsibility for them;

- Replace mandated medical treatment laws with laws encouraging charity.   Imagine if restaurants were required to feed whoever walks in, regardless of ability to pay, like doctors are.   Prices would go through the roof & waiting times would become ridiculous, just like in medical care.   Instead of assuming that everyday Americans are heartless & need laws to force us to care for the sick, let's encourage charitableness & protect doctors from lawyers' greed.

☐ Lawyers. I recall once reading about a maker of electronics for light aircraft that was told to pay a $20,000 settlement due to a plane crash. The crash had nothing to do with the plane's electronics at all. Yet, the owner was told that if he fought the settlement, it would cost more than the $20,000 -- & he might lose. Paying off was the smart, simple & wrong thing. But it's what happened, because of "joint & several damages".   This injustice has let lawyers sue everyone remotely connected to a case, & if there is a judgment for the plaintiff, the defendants pay -- are looted, really -- based on how much money they have, not how much guilt they bear.   Joint & several liability should be limited to cases where responsibility cannot be disentangled; judgement should be proportional to liability, not proportional to loot-ability. Also, the loser in a lawsuit

copyright 2016 © J. M. Payne

should pay the costs. To protect the ability of the poor, who might not pursue legitimate cases for fear of "loser pays", then, bonds to cover this risk should be available. Ambulance chasers & frivolous lawsuit filers would pay higher rates for these bonds, like a driver with a lots of accidents pays more for auto insurance. If the cost of the bond itself is too daunting, then the lawyer who believes he has a good case can provide the bond pro bono. This protects the poor while discouraging profiteering lawsuits.

☐ Judges. It seems to me that much of the mischief in the courts comes from judges & lawyers being too collegial. When a lawyer brings a frivolous but lucrative case before a judge, they may well share the same alma mater, fraternity, & other professional connections. Can the lawyer in a judge's robes be trusted to prevent his fellow lawyer from making a buck, or rather, a lot of bucks? Appaently not. Lawyers & judges should have completely separate career paths, because they have completely different jobs. Clients in lawyers' waiting room are paying those high hourly rates, not serve justice, but to win. A judge's job is precisely the opposite, to impartially uphold the law. The joy of a judge should be that lawyers leave his courtroom frustrated. So then, let judges have a different curriculum in school, separate fraternities & sororities, separate professional associations, separate career tracks & let them fight the lawyers, instead of facilitating them.

☐ Religion. Spiritual renewals -- Great Awakenings -- have driven social & political reforms in our past. I pray that today another Awakening is underway, because we can't afford to be asleep anymore. Houses of worship must return to caring for the poor, because we're likely to have more of them, as the bill comes due for our worshipping the idol we've made of government. Jesus said, "By this shall all men know that you are my disciples, that you have love one for another." It is also clearly commanded: "Pure and undefiled religion before God and the Father is this: to visit orphans and widows in their trouble, and to keep oneself unspotted from the world". Believers must leave off playing church & regrow the community that comes from undertaking these difficult tasks, for love's sake. Truth must also be renewed. Before the American Revolution, the "Black Robed Regiment" of America's preachers laid the foundations for liberty & then during the Revolution, fought for what they'd preached. Today, if America's preachers won't challenge the modern idolatry of Big Government, how will people's hearts be turned from politicians back to God?

☐ Money. Currently the value of our dollar is set by the whim of a quasi-governmental entity, the Federal Reserve System. Politicians

copyright © 2016 J. M. Payne

have used the ability to create money to, in effect, counterfeit our own currency, to pay for continuing their positions & privileges. Switching to gold or silver would be better, but the supply of precious metals doesn't change with population or prosperity. So, it seems to me that a better long term solution would be to peg the currency supply to the number of citizens. After all, the basic purpose of money is to provide citizens with a stable medium for the exchange of value. The Constitution already calls for a regular census. Amend it to tie the money supply to the number of citizens, at a ratio set by law & changeable only by a roll-call vote of Congress. People, not things, are what are truly valuable -- shouldn't money reflect that? When the population goes up, the need for currency goes up, the supply of currency will go up. Prices remain stable & politicians are denied the opportunity to manipulate money for their own ends.

☐ Race. The idea of race was invented by oppressors to divide & conquer us. There is only one race: the human race. I am of anglo stock, my wife is a lovely latina, my children, who are all adopted, are have afro, anglo, asian & latino heritages. Collectivists would say we are mixed-race; the truth is, we are members of the human race. Collectivists would say we are multi-ethnic; the truth is, we are American. Collectivists would reduce us to categories to be shoved into politically "correct" pigeonholes. We're not going into their pigeonholes; my children's futures are not be their pigeonholes; the American Dream isn't in their pigeonholes. Once & for all, let's burn our damnable race cards & begin treating each other as children of God & fellow citizens.

The dysfunction in our society goes deep -- into our attitudes, feelings, & habits of though & speech -- far beyond the reach of mere politics. But politics is like the roof of a house; if the roof is sagging, our 1st task is to shore it up so that it doesn't fall on our heads. So, we will next address the political structure & fundamental laws. Some of the ideas that follow might be good as is, others may spark better ones, & the rest will stay on these pages. This is perfectly fine; engineers know that good ideas are found only by sorting through a lot of bad ones. This task goes better with teamwork. As King Solomon advised, "Without counsel, plans go awry, But in the multitude of counselors they are established." The same person can produce both good & bad ideas. Thomas Paine, whose pamphlet "Common Sense" was a catalyst for the American Revolution, would later write "Age of Reason", sparking stiff rebukes from John Adams & Ben Franklin. Franklin wrote to Paine "...the consequence of printing this piece will be, a great deal of odium drawn upon yourself, mischief to you, and no benefit to others....burn this piece before it is seen by any other person." Paine would also enthusiastically

copyright 2016 © J. M. Payne

embrace the French Revolution, which was as catastrophic as the American Revolution was successful. Therefore, I am unwilling to trust my own, or anyone's, preconceived plans. Free people chart their own futures; subject populations timidly accept the course prepared by their owners. We, the people, must do the work of being free.

> **The dysfunction in our society goes deep -- into our attitudes, feelings, & habits of though & speech -- far beyond the reach of mere politics.**

Now, the legitimate purpose of laws is to place boundaries on power, both the government's & the people's. Since power tends to corrupt, the greater the power, the more robust the constraint required. Politicians, through government, wield great power over others, but individuals' power tends to be limited to their own lives. Wisdom says that the discretion & interpretation allowed to those entrusted with greater power must be limited. Too many laws, however, are written to magnify instead of minimize power. For example, so-called "hate crime legislation" allows officials to interpret the same crime differently, based on the presumed state of the criminal's heart. Equality before the law is replaced by political calculation. This is the old injustice of Jim Crow dressed up in fancy new clothes, & no longer bound by skin color, but freed to favor or oppress as the political winds blow.

Another example of wrong wording is this recent change to Florida's Constitution, regarding legislative districts (Article III, Section 20.a): "No apportionment plan or district shall be drawn with the intent to favor or disfavor a political party or an incumbent; and districts shall not be drawn with the intent or result of denying or abridging the equal opportunity of racial or language minorities to participate in the political process or to diminish their ability to elect representatives of their choice." The 1st deception is slyly slipped in by the word "intent." What intent lays behind any district's new boundaries is speculation. "Intent" simply frees politicians to demagog against whatever districts they don't like. The phrase "intent or result" that comes later is no better. How exactly do we correlate the "participation" of racial or language minorities to lines on a map? Since voting is not mandated, voter participation can't be controlled by district boundaries. And, which groups, exactly, are selected to be "racial or language minorities" for this purpose? If a statewide minority is a majority in a particular district, are members of the statewide majority in that district considered a minority for the drawing of that district? How do we count people who are multiracial, bilingual or multi-ethnic? How do we know who the "representatives of their choice are", if it's not the candidates who win the elections? Shall the State of Florida hire a team of psychics

copyright © 2016 J. M. Payne

to mystically sense who the voters really wanted, instead of who won the elections? (I offer what I think is a better approach to redistricting in proposal 18, below.)

> **Power tends to corrupt, so the greater the power, the more robust the constraint required.**

A final example of a badly written law is a recent tax increase in my own County: "Shall Seminole County District ad valorem millage be increased by up to one mill beginning July 1, 2013, and ending not more than four (4) fiscal years later on June 30, 2017, for essential operating expenses to: preserve 'A' rated academic, vocational, arts, and athletic programs; retain highly qualified teachers: and repair and maintain school buildings with annual reporting to the county's citizens to ensure fiscal stewardship of the funds?" First, consider the phrase "up to one mill"; we were not plainly told the price tag of what we were being sold. Then note, "essential operating expenses". Who decides what "essential" is? Observe that the word "retain" & not "hire" is used, so that not one new teacher need be added to the payroll. And, how do we know that these teachers are "highly qualified"? Did the District previously hire under qualified teachers, but now that will change? "Annual reporting" will be by whom & by what means, specifically? What is the threshold by which we know that "fiscal stewardship" has been achieved? What happens if it is not, & who is accountable? We are supposed to trust the politicians to do what's best. We would do better to heed Thomas Jefferson, who in the Kentucky Resolves of 1798 advised us, "In questions of powers, then, let no more be heard of confidence in man, but bind him down from mischief by the chains of the Constitution." But politicians through the years, have slipped from those chains with an oily dexterity that would put Houdini to shame. Once free of their chains, they set their minds to mischief, & that mischief is to put chains on us.

copyright 2016 © J. M. Payne

BREACHING of the BILL of RIGHTS

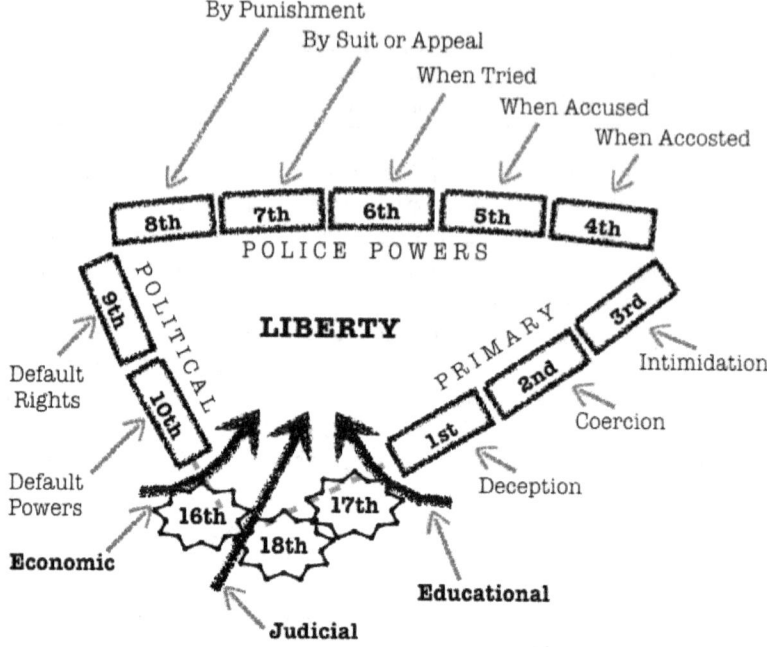

The Founders protected Liberty well, but not perfectly.

Think of Liberty as being at the summit of a hill with 3 sides, as shown in the figure. The slopes are open, grassy & not too steep; a nice place for a picnic. Although Liberty is on the high ground, it is not a natural fortification. To capture it, an enemy can come up one or more of the 3 slopes. The most obvious route is through the abuse of police powers, because the tools that government needs to maintain order, are also readily converted to overthrow our rights. The Stanford Prison Experiment is sobering evidence of how easily people can abuse power. A less direct strategy is to use deception, coercion & intimidation to attack Liberty's roots. These methods tend to be obvious & offensive, & so arouse opposition. The longest way up Liberty's hill is by undermining the political structures. An enemy quietly reengineers the machinery of government to rig the game from the inside, so that they always win. This allows the appearance of self-government to be maintained, even while its structure is being compromised, & reduces the chance of awakening resistance.

The Founders were well aware of these vulnerabilities of Liberty. That's why, before the ink was dry on the Constitution, plans were in motion

copyright © 2016 J. M. Payne

for fortifications to defend Liberty -- a Bill of Rights. These Amendments seem to me to be organized into 3 defensive lines guarding the 3 approaches up our hill. Now, the the defenses are well built, but not flawless. Those who dream of absolute power have had over 200 years to find, make, & exploit gaps in those defenses -- & they have. The full text of the Bill of Rights is provided in the Appendix, with other documents of interest, for easy reference. Let's look in more detail at these defenses & how they were breeched.

> **"In questions of powers, then, let no more be heard of confidence in man, but bind him down from mischief by the chains of the Constitution." -- Thomas Jefferson**

The 1st, 2nd & 3rd Amendments protect against primary threats to our liberties, from government deceiving, coercing & intimidating us:

1st Amendment - Deception: If politicians can deceive us, they can control us preemptively. By controlling the public conversation -- establishing a State church & denying religious freedom; suppressing free speech; monopolizing the news; regulating our associations; & restricting criticism of the government -- then the hard questions will never be asked & the only answers ever allowed will the ones that serve the official agenda.

2nd Amendment - Coercion: If politicians can monopolize firearms, they can literally put guns to our heads to force our obedience. Tyranny doesn't get any simpler than that. (This Amendment has nothing to do with hunting or sports -- no one was worried about the threat of tyrannical deer enslaving us or that we'd lose the country for lack of target shooting competitions.)

3rd Amendment - Intimidation: If the government's agents can come into our homes, eat our food, sleep in our beds, put their boots up on our coffee tables & leer at our teenage daughters, then what can they not do? This is winning by intimidation. Intimidation gets us used to letting government get away with whatever it wants. It is also an "unfunded mandate" -- if government needs an army, then it should provide barracks & mess halls, not quarter its troops in our houses.

The 4th through 8th Amendments are bulwarks against abuse of police powers, the courts & the penal system:

4th Amendment - Accosting: When accosting us for search or seizure, the government's agents are required to have good reason: probable cause, or an affidavit-backed warrant specifically describing the objectives of the search.

copyright 2016 © J. M. Payne

5th Amendment: - Accusation: When accusing us of a crime the government must have an indictment from a grand jury; it cannot come after us repeatedly for the same offense; it cannot compel us to testify against ourselves; & if it seizes our property, it must be after due process & with fair compensation.

6th Amendment - Trial: When trying us in court, the government must do it promptly, in public view, & without shopping for a compliant venue; it cannot have secret charges or secret witnesses; it must compel our witnesses to come to court; & it must provide us legal counsel.

7th Amendment - Suit & Appeal: When government fails to convict in criminal court, they can file a civil suit, but even then, the right to trial by jury is maintained; & if they try to evade a verdict by appealing to a higher court, those appeals are limited to questions only of law & not of fact.

8th Amendment - Punishment: If the government cannot get the conviction it wants, it is prohibited from getting a lesser conviction & then applying a cruel & unusual punishment, or setting excessive fines or bail.

The 9th & 10th Amendments guard against political undermining of our rights or preempting of our powers:

9th Amendment - Rights: By default, human rights belong to humans, not government.   Government cannot say that if the Constitution doesn't specifically protect a right, then it is free to infringe it.

10th Amendment - Powers: By default, political powers belong to the people, or the States individually.   Government cannot say that just because the Constitution doesn't specifically deny it a certain power, then the government is free to exercise it.

So we have completed our brief tour of Liberty's defenses. While those who love control have assaulted these defenses at various points, with varying degrees of success, they have been most effective in driving a wedge between the 1st Amendment, on the one hand, & the 9th & 10th Amendments on the other.   This requires some explanation.   Three explosions were set off by the Progressives in the early 20th century -- the 16th, 17th & 18th Amendments -- that were key to breaking through our defenses.   Then 3 wedges -- educational, economic & judicial -- were & are still being used to exploit the openings.

16th Amendment - Federal income tax: Sold to us as a tax that would only touch the ultra-rich, the income tax has made the IRS the most familiar -- & feared -- arm of Federal power.   Taxing people's incomes

copyright © 2016 J. M. Payne

directly gave the Federal government the financial leverage it needed to become the dominant player in the American economy.

17th Amendment - Direct election of Senators: Sold to us as a way to combat corruption in the choosing of Senators, the real effect of eliminating the States' power to select their Senators was to free the Federal government to be as big -- & bad -- as it wants to be.

18th Amendment - Prohibition of alcohol: Considered to be a failure because it was repealed, & because it gave America organized crime, in fact, this Amendment accomplished its purpose, which was to validate direct Federal intrusion into people's daily lives. Consider that 100 years ago, to ban the use of the "recreational chemical", alcohol, the Federal government needed a Constitutional Amendment. Today, it bans over 300 "controlled substances". Where is the Constitutional authority for that, since the 18th Amendment was repealed? Prohibition gave us organized crime & it centralized government to fight it, but its repeal ended neither.

Merely making an opening in the Constitutional guards against government dominance of society didn't achieve the fundamental transformation Collectivists fervently desire, of course. The breech had to be followed up with campaigns to extend control into every corner of our lives:

Educational wedge: The 1st Amendment prohibits political control in 5 areas: religion, speech, media, associations & redress of grievances. But one vital area was missed: education. We won't tolerate politicians interfering in the the 5 listed areas, but we meekly accept their monopolization of the schools. If you were granted total control of the press & houses of worship in a society, but I controlled the schools, then I submit that in a generation, my ideas will be preached from your pulpits & proclaimed in your media. For what is taught in the schools in one generation, becomes the conventional wisdom in the next. This, not efficiency nor excellence, is the agenda behind the consolidation of school systems. A century ago, the US had roughly 120,000 school districts in a population of about 100 million; today, with a population of over 300 million, we have only 15,000 districts. This is a 24-fold increase in centralization & with it came a terrible increase in ignorance. In a recent survey by the Annenberg Public Policy Center, only 38% of adults could name all three branches of government; only half knew that a 2/3 majority in Congress is needed to override a Presidential veto; & a mere 37% understood that a decision of the Supreme Court cannot be appealed. Prayer was removed from schools, not to protect children from the worship of God, but to prepare them for the worship of government. President Carter's creation of the Department of Education, President Bush's No Child Left Behind

copyright 2016 © J. M. Payne

program & most recently, Common Core standards, are the result of the enemies of Liberty overrunning our schools. They may have the best of intentions, but they are operating from the flawed mental model that government knows best. For more on how the schools have undermined education, see John Taylor Gatto's book, "Dumbing Us Down". Proposals 12, 15 & 16 below, would tend to push back this wedge.

Economic wedge: Article 1, Section 8 of of the Constitution gives Congress the power "To regulate Commerce with foreign Nations, & among the several States, & with the Indian Tribes" & "To make all Laws which shall be necessary & proper for carrying into Execution the foregoing Powers..." These are the "Commerce" & "Necessary & Proper" clauses.   A long train of court rulings, most notoriously Wickard vs Filburn in 1942, have commandeered the Commerce clause to empower the Federal government to regulate, well ... everything. We now have a

> **A Constitution, if it's only ink & paper, can never be a living Constitution. It is only a living Constitution when it lives in the hearts & minds of the people.**

70,000-plus page tax code which no one understands & which therefore can be manipulated for anything politicians want (like harassing the President's enemies). Government's uncontrolled spending, taxing & borrowing have left our nation at the mercy of regulators & creditors. Naive local politicians 1st accept Federal money, & then find they must obey Federal dictates or lose the funding on which they have come to depend. Amity Shlaes', "The Forgotten Man", lays out the human cost of politicians running the economy during the Great Depression, the worst economic time in American history -- so far. Proposals 1, 7, 8, 9, 19 & 20 below, are some ideas directed to these issues.

Judicial wedge: Unaccountability of judges was warned of by the Founders.   "Brutus", the nom-de-plume of a writer during the Ratification debates for our Constitution said, in Anti-Federalist 11, "The judicial power will operate to effect, in the most certain, but yet silent and imperceptible manner ... an entire subversion of the legislative, executive and judicial powers of the individual states." His fears began to be realized in the 1803 Marbury v. Madison decision, when the Supreme Court claimed the power of final Constitutional interpretation. Thomas Jefferson's reaction to this was that the Constitution "... meant that its co-ordinate branches should be checks on each other. But the opinion which gives to the judges the right to decide what laws are constitutional, and what not, not only for themselves in their own sphere of action, but for the legislature and executive also in their spheres, would make the judiciary a despotic branch." In case after case -- Dred Scott v. Sandford, Plessy v. Ferguson, Wickard v. Filburn,

copyright © 2016 J. M. Payne

Korematsu v. United States, Everson v. Board of Education, Abington Township School District v. Schempp, Brown v. Board of Education, Roe v. Wade, Kelo v. New London, & National Federation of Independent Business v. Sebelius -- the Supreme Court has imposed its will, sometimes for good, sometimes for bad. The unaccountability of the courts has enabled Collectivists to apply leverage to drive the other 2 wedges deeper into Liberty's defenses. The fulcrum for the lever is the doctrine of "selective incorporation" -- the practice of cherry-picking phrases from the Constitution & applying them out of context. It has effectively overturned the 9th & 10th Amendments, acting as a license for the Federal government to reach into anything it wants. The book, "Men in Black", by Mark Levin develops this subject fully. Proposals 11, 12, 13 & 16, are concepts to address this problem.

The proposals below are offered as ways to shore up our Constitution's defenses, for it cannot defend itself. A Constitution confined to ink & paper is not a living Constitution. It is only a living Constitution when it lives in the hearts & minds of the people. Its meaning cannot be defined by an elite; it belongs to all of us, or none of us. Therefore, we all have to turn from minding our own business to minding this political business; we must take time from pursuing our own happiness now, to secure the future happiness of our children. The old strategy of begging & pleading for politicians to behave has failed, as Congress' low approval & high reelection rates show. They are too insulated & arrogant to listen to us anymore. So, we must shift to a new strategy of reducing their power to behave badly. Such fundamental change in our political structures requires amending our Constitutional structures. Function ultimately follows form, & the form of this political system is now so corrupted that no reform that relies on the Establishment's consent can possibly succeed. Washington cannot save us; it cannot even save itself.

Thanks to the foresight of George Mason, a delegate to the Constitutional Convention, our Constitution contains a provision for our current situation: Article 5. It says, "The Congress, ... on the Application of the Legislatures of two thirds of the several States, shall call a Convention for proposing Amendments, which ... shall be valid to all Intents and Purposes, as Part of this Constitution, when ratified by the Legislatures of three fourths of the several States, or by Conventions in three fourths thereof, as the one or the other Mode of Ratification may be proposed by the Congress." This Article allows the people to to amend the Constitution directly, without interference from Congress, the President or the Courts. It is the final safety mechanism against a runaway government. There are well-meaning people who fear that this will be a "runaway" Convention that will annihilate the Constitution instead of restore it. Collectivists have already been doing that for decades, without any Convention. As to outcomes of a

copyright 2016 © J. M. Payne

Convention for proposing Amendments, it seems to me that we have 4 possible paths:

1. The Convention produces a slate of mostly bad Amendments & 3/4 of the States ratify most of them. If we live in a country that would propose & ratify such Amendments, then Liberty is already dead. A Convention would make no difference.

2. The Convention produces a slate of mostly bad Amendments but the States mostly refuse to ratify them. The ratification debates would wake millions of Americans up. And if America stays asleep, Liberty has no chance of surviving.

3. The Convention produces a slate of mostly good Amendments but the States mostly fail to ratify them. It would be disturbing that Collectivism's grip on the public debate is strong enough to block ratification, but those debates would still wake up millions. If America is awake, Liberty at least has a fighting chance.

4. The Convention produces a slate of mostly good Amendments & the States ratify most of them. These Amendments would go a long way towards restoring our liberties & restraining the government, & the ratification debates would wake up millions of Americans. This is a win-win for Liberty.

This Convention must produce a concise set of proposed Amendments, focused on shoring up the damage done to our Constitution, & able to be quickly debated & ratified. I apprehend that there two intertwined priorities for this set of Amendments. One is to stop the government's financial bleeding, the other, to roll back its centralization of power. If we fail to do the 2nd, the 1st will have only temporary effect. Now, I do not presume to have all the answers; as an engineer, I fully understand that to get one good idea, we must come up with & discard many others. So, the proposals listed here are wide ranging & intended to promote discussion. Some are my own, others borrowed, & several parallel Mark Levin's "The Liberty Amendments". They are listed in the order that their effect is encountered in the Federal Constitution, with those applicable at State &/or Federal levels reserved to the end. Proposed additions are <u>underlined</u> & deletions struck-through.

1. Because Congress has abdicated its Constitutional duties for legislating to the Executive, Judicial, or administrative branches, then referring to Article 1, Section 1: "Congress shall not delegate its power & duty to legislate, in fact nor effect, to the Executive or Judicial, or any subsidiary agency; & Federal criminal offenses shall consist only of violations of laws passed by Congress."

copyright © 2016 J. M. Payne

2. Because Congress's bundling of unrelated laws into omnibus bills has subverted the Presidential veto & perverted legislative priorities, & to prevent the excess accumulation of laws, to ensure their regular maintenance & to moderate the influence of special interests, then referring to Article 1, Section 1: "Congress shall pass no law exceeding 4,500 words in length; each bill shall be engrossed for 120 days prior to its passage by Congress & shall not be amended during engrossment; for any bill to become law without engrossment shall require a 2/3 majority roll-call vote of Congress. Laws passed by a simple majority of Congress, & all regulations authorized thereby, shall become void after 7 years; if passed by at least a 2/3 majority, after 12 years; & if by at least a ¾ majority, after 17 years; reauthorization shall require a roll call vote by Congress on each bill separately, with the term of the reauthorization subject to the same provision regarding majorities; & this Amendment shall be retroactive on all Federal laws upon ratification." (4,500 words is roughly 10 pages of text, or about the length of the entire Constitution as originally written; this is about half again the 3,100 word average length for bills passed in recent Congresses.)

3. Since it is a conflict of interest for those who practice law to make law, then referring to Article 1, Section 2, Clause 2 & Section 3, Clause 3: "No person practicing law, or a registered lobbyist, shall be eligible to become a Representative or Senator until a time equal to the term of the office being sought shall have passed; nor shall a Representative or Senator practice law, or be a registered lobbyist after leaving office until a time equal to the term of the office held shall have passed."

4. As political careerism tends to diminish the people's representation & promote elitism among elected officials, then, referring to Article 1, Section 2, Clause 2 & Section 3, Clause 3: "A Representative or Senator may be reelected to a 2nd consecutive term only by earning a simple majority of the vote, & for consecutive terms thereafter, by a 3/5th majority; should the incumbent not earn the required majority, then a run-off election shall be held between the two remaining candidates with the most votes each; & if there is only one other candidate besides the incumbent, then a new election shall be held, for which the incumbent shall not be eligible."

5. As the representation of our People has been diluted by population growth, & the imbalance between large & small States has plagued our politics since the Founding, therefore revise Article 1, Section 2, Clause 3: "The Number of Representatives shall not exceed one for every thirty Thousand, but each State shall have at Least one

copyright 2016 © J. M. Payne

Representative;" becomes "The number of Representatives in Congress shall be 10 times the number of States, & apportioned by population; except, each State shall have at least one Representative, & no State shall be apportioned more than 20 Representatives; & Representatives not apportioned to a State for this reason shall be deducted from the total number of Representatives. States subject to this limitation may establish borders for new States, with the consent of the Legislatures involved; & each State so formed shall have 2 Senators." (In my estimation, perhaps 5 new States would be formed, from California, Texas, Florida, & New York. This would yield a House with 550 Representatives & a Senate with 110 members. It would also restore the ratio of representatives between the largest & average States to 2:1, the same as it was in the earliest Congresses, down from the current ratio of about 6:1.)

6. To restore the balance of power between the Federal & State governments, referring to Article 1, Section 3 (as changed by the17th Amendment, Clause 1): "The Senate of the United States shall be composed of two Senators from each State, elected by the people thereof, chosen by the Legislature thereof, for six years; & each Senator shall have one vote."

7. To limit to corruption of the Federal Commerce Clause, referring to Article I, Section 8, Clause 1: "The Congress shall have Power within the limits set forth in this Constitution to: lay & collect Taxes, Duties, Imposts & Excises, to pay the Debts & provide for the common Defense & general Welfare of the United States; & to regulate Commerce with foreign Nations, & among the several States, & with the Indian Tribes, only to the extent such commerce has a direct effect upon more than one State, or Tribe, or the Nation as a whole;"

8. Since there should be no taxation without illumination, as hidden taxation disguises the burden on our people & so frees politicians to increase that burden, then referring to Article 1, Section 9 (as changed by the 16th Amendment): "The Government shall collect only indirect taxes upon the incomes [or purchases] of the people themselves, besides Duties, Imposts & Excises; this tax rate shall be a one percentage rate with one exemption [or rebate] per person in dollars, with the single rate & exemption [or rebate] set by law & changeable only by a 2/3 roll-call vote of Congress; & no taxes shall be collected before their date due." (This prevents stealth sales taxes such as "corporate" or "value added" ones & prohibits tax withholding, that bizarre scheme of pre- & over-payment of taxes, which forces us to beg the government to return money to which it

copyright © 2016 J. M. Payne

had no right.   This proposal is worded as a simplification of the income tax; the wording in [ ] would be for a sales tax, like the Fair Tax.)

9. Because politicians clearly cannot be trusted with the power of discretionary currency, then referring to Article I, Section 8, Clause 5: "To coin Money, ~~regulate the Value thereof,~~ the value of which shall be at a fixed ratio to the number of citizens determined by the enumeration herein before directed to be taken, with such ratio being set by law & changeable only by a 2/3 majority roll-call vote of Congress, ..."

10. To clarify the working of the Electoral College, which exists to prevent the election of a special interest President, amend the State Constitutions, or the Federal Constitution, referring to Article 2, Section 1, Clause 3: "The Electors shall meet in their respective states and vote by ballot for President and Vice-President, one of whom, at least, shall not be an inhabitant of the same state with themselves; all Electors for President of each State shall cast their ballots for the winner of the popular vote in their respective Congressional districts; & the Electors corresponding to the Senators shall cast their ballots for the winner of the popular vote in their respective States."

11. Because the Judicial branch has become unaccountable to the people, then referring to Article 3, Section 1: "The Judges, both of the supreme and inferior Courts, shall hold their Offices during good Behavior & shall be impeached when Congress deems necessary; each year the longest-serving Justice of the Supreme Court shall retire & a new Justice shall be appointed, with the advice & consent of the Senate; all other Federal judges shall serve a term of 7 years, & may be reappointed once, subject to confirmation as provided by law; and Judges shall, at stated Times, receive for their Services a Compensation, which shall not be diminished during their Continuance in Office."

12. To provide a check upon the excesses of the Judicial branch, referring to Article 3, Section 1, add this Clause: "Within 2 years of a Supreme Court decision, Congress shall have the power to nullify that decision by 2/3 vote of the House & Senate; the President shall have the power to nullify, if sustained by a majority vote of Congress; the States shall have the power to nullify by concurring resolutions in 3/5 of their legislatures."

13. As it is not within the powers of the Federal Government to surrender the sovereignty of the People, then referring to Article 6, Clause 2 of the Federal Constitution, add: "In no case whatsoever

copyright 2016 © J. M. Payne

shall the provisions of any treaty of the United States nullify the protections of the People's rights nor the limitations on Federal powers set forth in this Constitution."

14. Since the Executive & Judicial branches of the Federal Government are as dangerous to liberty as the Legislative, revise the wording throughout the Bill of Rights from "Congress shall make no law..." to "The Federal Government shall not...".

15. Because education is far too important to be entrusted to politicians, add education to the 1st Amendment: "...respecting an establishment of religion, or prohibiting the free exercise thereof; or abridging the freedom of speech, or of education, or of the press; or the right of the people peaceably to assemble, and to petition the Government for a redress of grievances."

16. As "selective incorporation" flips the Constitution upside-down by empowering instead of limiting the Federal government & makes the Federal Courts into a de facto, ongoing Constitutional Convention, add an Amendment: "The Federal courts shall not use selective incorporation in applying this Constitution to cases, but shall respect the Constitutional context." (At the same time, each State should incorporate the Bill of Rights into their respective State Constitutions, to be applied & enforced by their State courts.)

17. As it is impossible to have a just society in which any group of people are defined as subhuman, to be disposed of at will, then either:

   17.a. Alter the 14th Amendment: "All persons ~~born or naturalized in the United States and~~ subject to the jurisdiction ~~thereof~~ of the United States, are, from the moment of their conception or naturalization, citizens of the United States and of the State wherein they reside...";

   17.b. Add a new Amendment: "Neither the United States nor any State shall deprive any human being, from the moment of conception, of life without due process of law; nor deny to any human being, from the moment of conception, within its jurisdiction, the equal protection of the laws." (Rep. Lawrence Hogan - R-MD)

18. As politicians have shown that they will draw the boundaries of legislative districts to ensure their re-election & not to best represent the people (aka "gerrymandering") a redistricting procedure is needed to mitigate political discretion, interpretation & favoritism. States should pass amendments or legislation requiring that the shapes of electoral districts within a jurisdiction to meet requirements based on the following metrics. Each proposed

copyright © 2016 J. M. Payne

district would be evaluated by these metrics & the arithmetic average for all the districts taken. Each metric is defined such that a larger value corresponds to greater likelihood of gerrymandering. No district shall be approved whose metric exceeds the average for all the districts for that metric by more than a fixed percentage, as set by law.

18.a. Excess Boundary: Gerrymandering requires a lot of boundary for the size of the district. Therefore, ratio of the length of the boundary of the district to the square root of its area. (The square root corrects for different population densities.)

18.b. Aspect Ratio: Gerrymandering tends to produce long, skinny districts. Therefore, ratio of longest distance between any two points in the district to the shortest length of a straight line dividing that district into halves of equal population, within 10%.

18.c. Discretionary Boundary: Gerrymandering generally has to ignore preexisting boundaries. Therefore, ratio the total discretionary boundary to the total boundary for the district. All boundaries shall be considered discretionary except those defined by law, such as: natural borders, (rivers, coastlines, etc.); jurisdictional boundaries, (city, & county borders, etc.); & artificial barriers (limited-access highways, canals, etc.).

19. Since politicians can spend faster than the people can earn, a Balanced Budget Amendment is needed, at State & Federal levels, that incorporates provisions like these:

19.a. Prohibits deficit spending, except in time of declared war or emergency as voted by a supermajority of the legislature;

19.b. Requires a supermajority for all tax increases;

19.c. Limits Government spending to a fixed percentage of the Gross Domestic (or State) Product;

19.d. For Federal, lays on each State, or for States, lays on each County or City, the responsibility for funding any deficit incurred, which does not meet the other requirements of the amendment, assessed in proportion to population,.

19.e. Provide that the legislators' salaries be held in escrow until they have passed a legitimate budget. Legislators shall borrow against the escrow in lieu of salary, until a budget is passed; & should a budget not be passed when due, the

copyright 2016 © J. M. Payne

escrow shall be withdrawn & each Legislator's debt against his or her account shall be payable immediately & in full.

20. Experience has made it clear that politicians cannot be trusted with wage & price controls, so add this amendment at the Federal &/or State level: "The Government shall not set wages, except for those persons in its own employ, nor set prices, except for goods or services it offers; & the Government shall not engage in collective bargaining with its employees."

21. To prevent special interests from taking advantage of voter apathy to enable a small fraction of the voters to impose their will on the majority, amend at the Federal &/or State level: "No candidate shall be elected, nor any referendum passed, unless turnout is at least 50% of the registered voters; if turnout is less than 50%, a new election shall be held; & if turnout is less than 50% in the 2nd election, then the office in question shall remain vacant until the next regular election, or the referendum shall be rejected."

Efforts are already underway to make the Convention of States happen. I highly recommend Mark Levin's excellent book, "The Liberty Amendments" for its through examination of twelve well thought out amendments & sound arguments for an Article 5 Convention.   On 7 December 2013, nearly 100 delegates from 32 States met at Mt. Vernon for an assembly, not to decide on amendments for consideration, but to decide on the structure for running the Convention. The Article V Caucus has over 100 State legislators signed up to uphold the principles of federalism and limited government with web-based information, model legislation & strategic meetings to encourage the States to adopt resolutions to call for an Article 5 convention.   There is also the Convention of the States Project which seeks to call a convention for a particular subject rather than a particular amendment, building a grassroots political operation in a minimum of 40 states, getting 100 people to volunteer in at least 75% of the State legislative districts. The Coolidge Project is also working to elect State legislators who will refuse the bribe of Federal funding & restore federalism. The ultimate goal of all of these efforts is to shore up the breeches in the Constitution & restore the functioning of our Republic.

copyright © 2016 J. M. Payne

REINFORCING the BILL of RIGHTS

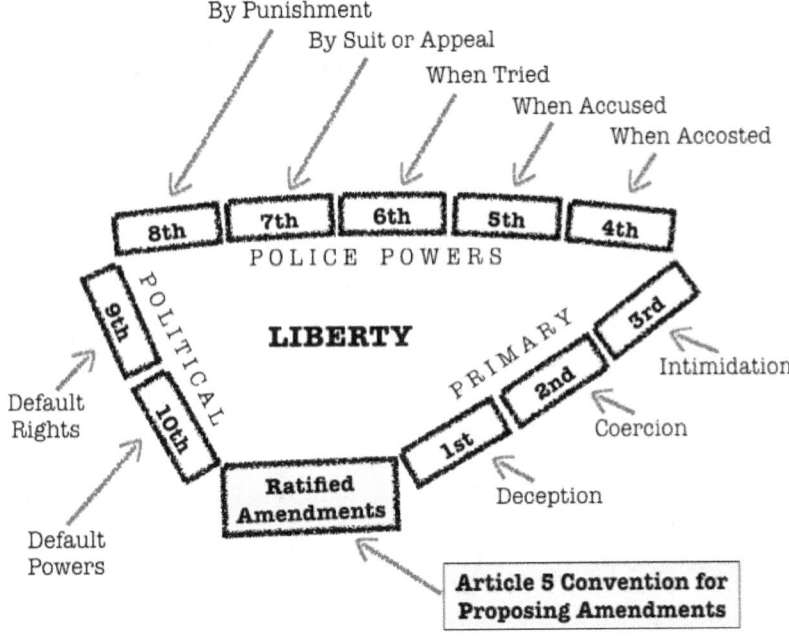

We can close the breech in Liberty's defenses.

How closing the breech the Constitution's defenses would look, in terms of Liberty's Hill, is illustrated in this figure. It is a vast improvement on our current, unsustainable condition. But a static defense is ultimately just a delayed defeat. The Constitution only lives when it lives in the hearts & minds of our people, when every citizen is a scholar & defender of it. Only then does it really belong to all of us. The appetite of Collectivism won't disappear. We will have to defend the revitalized Constitution. We will have to seek further Amendments to deal with counter moves. But, let's say several years along, we've succeeded in restoring the Constitutional structure. What then? The $19 Trillion (by then $22 or $28 Trillion?) Federal debt will still hang over us. Tens of millions of Americans will still depend for their daily bread on a government that's broke. Families & communities will not have been healed by the ratification of Amendments. As setting a broken leg does not heal the bone, but makes healing possible, so these political repairs can't heal society, but can enable the healing process.

If all this seems overwhelming, consider the situation in the newly independent United States. The country was falling apart. Under the

copyright 2016 © J. M. Payne

Articles of Confederation, the debt from the Revolution could not be retired. Trade was stalled between States. There was Shay's Rebellion. Then we had a Constitutional Convention that completely re-engineered the government, followed by an almost two year long ratification battle. This was followed by the Whiskey Rebellion. Politically, America was a mess. And yet, the tumult soon subsided, & the new nation began to thrive, because people were free & society's success did not depend on government "running the country".

Suppose we succeed in restoring the government to its Constitutional boundaries. What then?

So let us no longer hope for a political salvation. A total renewal - spiritual, social, cultural & political - is needed. It has happened in America before, in the Great Awakenings of 1730's & again in the early 1820's. Some would claim that the decline of traditional religious denominations means that faith is fading in America. But I believe this is the prelude to a new birth of belief, for new wine cannot go into old wineskins. Books like "The Forgotten Ways: Reactivating the Missional Church" by Alan Hirsch & Frank Viola's "Finding Organic Church: A Comprehensive Guide to Starting and Sustaining Authentic Christian Communities", discuss how churches can face the future by returning to their roots. Only when we reclaim the truth, can we speak truth to power. To Collectivists, who view government as a god, we say: "Render to Caesar the things that are Caesar's, and to God the things that are God's". To Conservatives, seeking security behind walls, we say: "Whoever seeks to save his life will lose it, and whoever loses his life will preserve it". To the Establishment, clinging to their cronyism, we say: "Extortion turns wise people into fools, and bribes corrupt the heart". To moderates, trusting compromise to avoid conflict, we say: "Pay careful attention, then, to how you walk — not as unwise people but as wise - making the most of the time, because the days are evil." King Solomon, that wisest of men, taught us that there is "nothing new under the sun". We can thrive again, if we remember the 1st things. Our possibilities can be bigger than our problems, if we have the courage for the "animating contest of freedom".

copyright © 2016 J. M. Payne

V. ON THE POSSIBILITIES OF LIBERTY

"There is no end which the human will despairs of attaining through the combined power of individuals united into a society .... In the United States associations are established to promote the public safety, commerce, industry, morality, & religion." - Alexis de Tocqueville, Democracy in America, Book I, chapter 12

On 25 January 2012, in Cedar Rapids, Iowa, at the Conveyor Engineering & Manufacturing plant, the President of the United States offered up this dull, gray vision of America: "Folks don't have unrealistic ambitions; they do believe that if they work hard they should be able to achieve that small measure of an American Dream. That's what this country is about. That's what you deserve." Compare that to Thomas Paine's confident declaration in 1776: "It is not in numbers, but in unity, that our great strength lies; yet our present numbers are sufficient to repel the force of all the world" ("Common Sense, Chapter IV"). How is it that an Englishman, only a year in the newly independent America, struggling in the shadow of the British Empire, saw in us the strength to "repel the force of all the world", yet a President today can say that all we deserve, all we can hope for, is "that small measure of an American Dream"?

To see what's wrong with this failure of vision, we need only consult the most truthful members of society -- children. A little boy will tell you that when he grows up, he's going to be President; he will not tell you he dreams of being elected Clerk of the Courts. A little girl might tell you she's set her sights on becoming an astronaut; not about her plan for becoming an aerospace technician. Yet, if it happens that the boy ends up as a Clerk of the Courts & the girl becomes a technician (or the other way round), they are unlikely to be bitter. This is the paradox of the American Way: we have big dreams, & yet are not discontented with our real achievements. This is a powerful preventive against tyranny, as tyrants need for people's discontents to be large & their dreams, small.

Tyranny springs from Lord Acton's maxim, "Power tends to corrupt, and absolute power corrupts absolutely". A clue to how power corrupts is found in the curious saying, "Don't shoot the messenger!" If an organization receives a message of a routine problem, & they will thank the messenger & deal it in their routine way. But certain messages will get the messenger shot. Since it's better to be informed than ignorant of a problem, why would anyone do this? Livingston's Law reveals the motive behind this madness. Livingston's Law, restated in my own words says:

copyright 2016 © J. M. Payne

An organization will react to a message of a problem that threatens its power structure by "shooting the messenger" & redacting all evidence of the message, initiating a self-reinforcing cycle of blindness & neglect that subverts all attempts at solution.

William L. Livingston's unusual book, "Have Fun at Work", is not an easy read; but if you are frustrated by the invincibility of bureaucratic stupidity, he explains it quite thoroughly. Livingston's Law activates in an organization when power eclipses purpose. Blindness is the 1st symptom of this corruption of power. Once in its grip, all the leadership can see is the need to maintain power. After that, disaster is just a matter of time.

If you think this is theoretical, consider the Titanic. She was not sunk by an iceberg; the iceberg was floating along minding its own business. She was sunk by her unsinkability. The mental model of her creators was that the worst thing that could happen to a large, oceangoing vessel was to collide with another large ship, & the worst place to be hit was at the junction between 2 watertight sections. The Titanic could have 4 of her watertight sections compromised & not sink, so she was "unsinkable". Unfortunately, ships are part of a larger system that included the moon, the sea -- & icebergs. A moonless night & a calm sea made icebergs hard to spot until it was too late to avoid collision. Titanic's sliding collision with the iceberg that opened 5 of her sections to the sea was not in her creators' thinking. The presumption of unsinkability prevented the precautions that might have saved the lives of 1500 people aboard Titanic.

> **The 1st surprise attack on Pearl Harbor was not 7 December 1941. It was 7 Feb 1932, nearly a decade earlier.**

Or consider a military case. The 1st surprise attack on Pearl Harbor was not 7 December 1941. It was 7 February 1932, nearly a decade earlier. It was launched from the aircraft carriers USS Lexington & USS Saratoga, under the command of Admiral Harry Yarnell, as part of a US naval exercise. His attack was a complete surprise & success, very much like the real Japanese one that was to come. But the admirals who'd built their careers on battleships, found it unthinkable that the ungainly "flat-top" aircraft carrier now ruled the seas. So, they decided they would edit reality to fit their preconceptions & glossed over the vulnerability that Admiral Yarnell demonstrated. Unfortunately, the Imperial Japanese Navy was not so closed-minded. So on a Sunday morning that will live in infamy, 2403 Americans paid with their lives for this failure of vision. (The fact that you've likely never heard of this appalling government failure is probably because government runs

copyright © 2016 J. M. Payne

most of the schools.)   In events as diverse as the fall of the Roman Empire, the tragic end of the Romanov dynasty, the response of the American auto industry to foreign competition & the accumulation of $19 Trillion in Federal debt, we have to ask, "How could those in charge not see disaster coming & do something?"   Because there are none so blind as those who will not see.

When an organization is young & mission oriented, power is sought to fulfill the mission.   As it gets older, the organization tends to become more important than its mission.   Power becomes its own justification, & this sets the trigger for Livingston's Law.   Livingston's Law is why our perennial attempts to curb bureaucratic "waste, fraud & abuse" produce little change.   The only effective way manage power is with structures that separate & balance power, so that abuse is less likely to occur & less damaging when it does.   When power is disbursed, cooperation & compromise are needed to get anything done,   which works against abuses of power.   When there is an abuse of power, the damage tends to be contained because the other competing powers guard their prerogatives. Competition acts as a shield against tyranny.

Therefore, if America is to again realize the possibilities of liberty, the structures of power must again be separated, balanced & scaled down, so that Livingston's Law is not continually violated, as it is now.   But that is not enough. We live in a world of complex, challenging problems. Simply dismantling the unworkable, centralized structures of political control will not solve those problems.   There still needs to be the means for people to solve, or at least mitigate, them. This answer is found in "Ashby's Law of Necessary Variety" (as quoted by Livingston in his book, "Friends in High Places"):

> "Only variety in the control system can deal with variety in
> the system controlled."

To provide the diversity of control needed to cope with the complex system of American society, there are two basic strategies being applied in America today.   One, which brought America from a collection of former colonies to a world superpower, is embraced by Conservatives. The other, now being imposed on us by Collectivists, is taking us all off a cliff.

Collectivism's prescription for problem of Ashby's Law is to hyper-empower about 6 or 7 million politicians & bureaucrats to make the important decisions for over 320 million Americans.   This approach fails in 3 ways: information, intelligence, & interest.   The information problem is simply a lack of bandwidth.   The relatively small group making decisions simply can't access & process information in the quantities & at the speeds needed.   This, more than corruption or even

copyright 2016 © J. M. Payne

laziness, is why government programs aren't "fast, flexible & efficient". Even if we could hardwire civil servants to the internet to get the information into their heads, we still have the 2nd problem: intelligence. Government officials aren't any smarter than the rest of us. Even with all the necessary information, they will still make mistakes & those mistakes will be amplified by the power they wield.   But let's further suppose that the government hires only certified geniuses, these geniuses consent to having their brains hardwired to the internet & that they are collectively smart enough to achieve the Greater Good. We still have a 3rd, fatal problem: how do we know that this wired-in, super-smart elite will make decisions for the Greater Good?   What if they decide their own good is more important than ours?   On what grounds would we question this techno-politico-elite's judgements?   We would have none. We would be at their mercy. Collectivism's answer to this is more procedures & funding.   But experience shows the ever-bigger bureaucracy wallows comfortably in procedures & soaks up funding. Like a real-life Dr. Frankenstein, we would find that our creation has become our master -- or our nemesis. The government-centric approach is simply not a viable control system for any America in which we want to live.

> **On what grounds would we question this techno-politico-elite's judgements? We would have none.**

Conservatism's response to Ashby's Law is to look to Liberty to deal with the control problem: 320 million Americans making most of their decisions for themselves.   We are each experts on our own circumstances, so we have the best (though not perfect) information for making our own decisions. We don't need to be smarter than everyone else, because we are generally smart enough for our own situations. Most importantly, because we must each live with the consequences, we each have a strong interest in making good decisions. Thus the needed information, intelligence & interest are aligned at the decision point. When our needs exceed our individual abilities, we use our freedom to form associations & create solutions.   As de Tocqueville described it, "The citizen of the United States is taught from infancy to rely upon his own exertions in order to resist the evils & the difficulties of life; he looks upon the social authority with an eye of mistrust & anxiety, & he claims its assistance only when he is unable to do without it. ...   If a stoppage occurs in a thoroughfare ... the neighbors immediately form themselves into a deliberative body; & this extemporaneous assembly gives rise to an executive power which remedies the inconvenience before anybody has thought of recurring to a pre-existing authority." This is a fast, flexible & viable control system for the complexities of a free society.

copyright © 2016 J. M. Payne

In fact, this is the system that produced America. Once upon a time, there were a baker's dozen of colonies strung out along an untamed coast. America was populated by the people the rest of the world didn't want -- religious fanatics, retired pirates, dream chasers, fugitives from the law, & people down to their last chance. All the Better Sort back home thought that they'd die in the far wilderness, & good riddance. But they did not die -- they thrived. They became the richest & most generous nation on earth. They purged their own society from slavery

> **America was populated by the people the rest of the world didn't want -- religious fanatics, retired pirates, dream chasers, fugitives from the law, & people down to their last chance.**

in a great war. They saved the world from totalitarianism, twice. That didn't happen because they were the sort to meekly follow government-issued 5-year plans. It didn't happen because they carefully followed standard operating procedures. It happened because these people, these Americans, had the liberty to experiment, to innovate, to fail & try again. They were free to create the control complexity demanded by Ashby's Law, & to reorganize themselves to avoid the trap of Livingston's Law. These laws of human nature describe the dynamics of how humans deal with complex problems. Many other societies have ignored them, relying instead on power, & they paid the price.

copyright 2016 © J. M. Payne

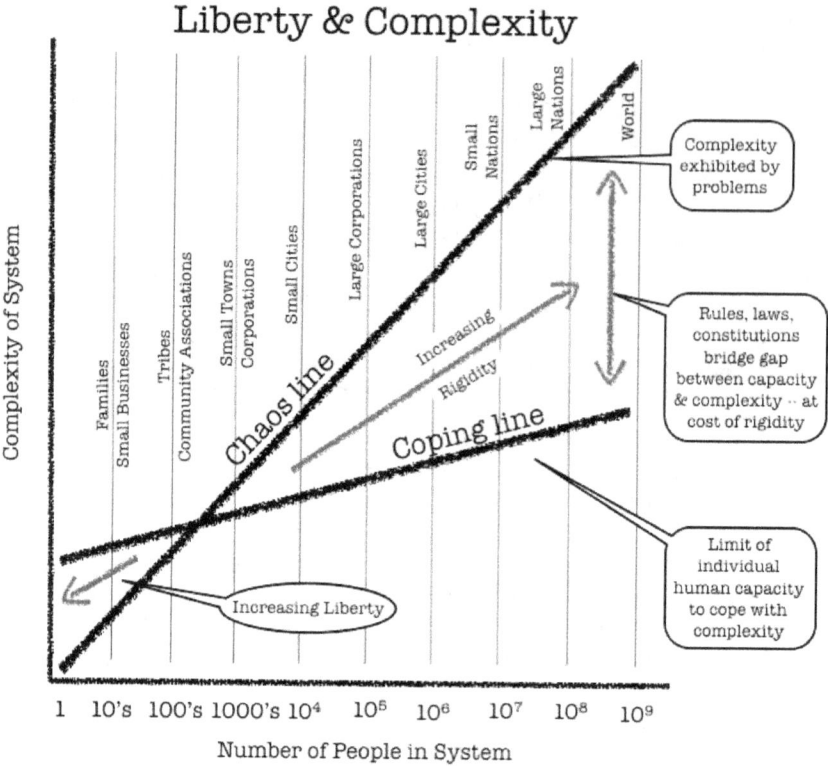

Number of People in System

Now, we can illustrate this relationship between liberty & complexity with two lines: one representing the challenge of chaos & one representing human capacity for coping, as shown in the figure. Problems falling above the chaos line are too big for a group of that size; those below the coping line are generally manageable. The regions between these lines are where politics come into play. Small is beautiful here because that's where freedom thrives. Big tends to be bad here because that's where government grows. Note in the figure how the chaos associated with the increasing size of groups grows faster than the group's ability to cope with that chaos. This is because it is a fundamental human limitation that we can only personally interact with a fairly limited number of people. Communication can't keep up with chaos. (I conceive that these lines are not fixed but will float & perhaps bend with different situations, cultures, & individuals.) Now, the difference between a mob & an army is that an army is organized; as groups get larger, organization bridges the gap between coping & chaos, but organizational controls impose rigidity. With more, smaller groups there are many leaders & therefore more control variety. Small, local associations like those described by de Tocqueville are able to gather Ashby knowledge, operate below the Livingston threshold & keep the

copyright © 2016 J. M. Payne

system from being hijacked by those whose priority is monopolizing power. There was a time in America when most decisions were made & most problems solved, by small, local groups, close to the situation, groups sized in the 10's to 100's of individuals. This, I perceive, is the region where the coping line is usually above the chaos line. But over time, decisions & power have been progressively centralized, until Washington, DC, quite literally decides what lightbulbs we can use in our homes, what our schoolchildren can eat for lunch, & who can use which bathroom. As laws & rules increase, this rigidity filters down into smaller & smaller groups, producing both misery & disaster. Misery, because the rigidity forces the coping line down, leaving people feeling frustrated & stripped of control. Disaster, because the rigidity also pushes the chaos line up as reality refuses to submit to its authority. For people to be able to adapt, improvise & overcome problems, most of the decisions & power have to fall in the region of the figure where the coping line is above the chaos line, typically groups of a few hundred or less. A society like this will be filled with many small, organic connections holding its fabric together, instead than the fewer, mechanistic ones of a politically centralized society.

> **It is a myth of Collectivism that, since scientists & engineers have become adept at manipulating nature, then politicians are free to manipulate human nature.**

For example, the curriculum standards being imposed on our nation's schools do not come from a professional teachers' organization. Instead, the National Association of Governors & a cabal of corporate interests have developed top-down curriculum standards called Common Core. In contrast to this approach, a century ago when steam boilers were exploding, killing & maiming people, engineers did not wait for politicians & corporations to establish standards. Instead, through the American Society of Mechanical Engineers, engineers developed the Boiler & Pressure Vessel Code. Boilers built to the Code didn't blow up. Over time, governments adopted the Code for boilers built in their jurisdictions. The people led, the politicians followed, problem solved.

Modern systems are not immune to political arrogance. Consider the loss of the Space Shuttles Challenger & Columbia. Congress decided that America's Space Transportation System could be built on the cheap, so money could be spent on priorities here on earth, like getting themselves reelected. So the tried-&-true vertical stack design, with the Orbiter on top & boosters below, was changed to the horizontal stack, with the Orbiter hanging off the side of that massive external fuel tank. And, for the 1st time on a space vehicle carrying people, solid-rocket boosters (SRB's) would be used, strapped to the side of that massive fuel

copyright 2016 © J. M. Payne

tank.   Challenger died because one of the SRB's failed; Columbia, because a chunk of thermal insulation came off of that fuel tank & punched a hole the Orbiter's wing.   Much has been written & said about the technical aspects of these disasters -- of o-rings & ice, of the composition & application of insulation -- but very little attention has been paid to the human arrogance that set the stage for the technical failures.   Where was the accountability for the politicians whose decisions put the Space Transportation System on a path to failure? Yet this same political system is now in control of our health insurance, through Washington's "pass-the-law-to-find-out-what's-in-it" process, giving us the so-called Affordable Care Act.   Many, many more lives are at risk through this political intrusion into health care than the 14 tragically lost in our Space Shuttles.

Of late, political interests have sought to seduce us into submission by claiming that the planet's ecosystem is going to be mortally damaged by human emissions of carbon dioxide.   Consider instead the threats (of varying likelihood) that really could take down our civilization:

☐ Electro-Magnetic Pulse (EMP), either by the deliberate detonation of a nuclear device in the upper atmosphere, or through a solar flare, like the Carrington Event in 1859, before we were so dependent on electrical technology.   (See "Guilty Knowledge" Frank Gaffney, Jr., for further information.)

☐ Eruption of one of the world's 6 active super-volcanoes, such as the Yellowstone super-volcano which would devastate America's mid-western breadbasket & affect global climate for decades.

☐ Pandemics of antibiotic-resistant bacterial, fungal or viral diseases, or genetically-engineered microbes.

☐ Meteor impacts have done immense damage to the planet in the past, & could do so again.

This table compares the scale of some of these events:

Event	Energy equivalent, TNT	Time	Effect
Chicxulub impact	96 million megatons	65 million years ago	K-T extinction (dinosaur-killer)
Barringer Crater	2.5 megatons	50,000 years ago	Crater 4,100 ft. across & 570 ft. deep

copyright © 2016 J. M. Payne

Event	Energy equivalent, TNT	Time	Effect
Mt. Tambora eruption	800 megatons	1815	1816 was the "Year without a summer", 71,000 deaths
Carrington Event	2.4×10^{17} megatons (?)	1859	Loss of national electric grids
Tunguska explosion	10 megatons	1908	830 square miles of forest flattened
Apophis asteroid	750 megatons	2036 (?)	Local devastation; global effects

The asteroid Apophis is an 820-ft, 25-million ton rock that will pass between the Earth & our Moon at more than 28,000 mph in April, 2029. It's more than 80 times bigger than the rock that made Meteor Crater in Arizona. Depending on its exact trajectory, it may or may not circle back to hit the earth in April, 2036. It if hits, it will release the energy of 50,000 Hiroshima bombs. The Mt. Tamobora volcanic eruption was about as powerful as the impact of Apophis would be; so the effects might be of a similar scale. Mt. Tambora killed tens of thousands locally & the following year, 1816, had no summer. This climate disruption caused famines around the planet, starving tens of thousands more. An impact by Apophis would be proportionately worse in our more populated world, & of course we have no guarantee that it would fall in a sparsely populated area, like Mt. Tambora & the Tunguska event.

As frightening as these events are, the Chicxulub impact that ended the dinosaurs' domination was more than 100,000 times worse. Yet Earth's biosphere survived. If 96 million megatons of catastrophe didn't kill the planet, why does anyone think that coal-fired power plants & SUV's will? Because control of energy means control of people. We ignore, or are willfully blind to, more serious threats that provide only limited opportunity for political control, like natural or man-made EMP. A full discussion of EMP & its consequences is beyond this work, but the damage to our power grids could take years to fully repair. Could our civilization survive such a disruption?

The fact is, the idea of human-caused climate change is a modern superstition, invented to justify more centralized control, & accepted because it feels better to believe that we are to blame, than to believe that things are out of our control. We are living in a glass palace of centralized control, beautiful & brittle. Any major disaster could

copyright 2016 © J. M. Payne

shatter it; even much smaller crises could start the crack that ends with the whole edifice in a pile of broken glass. Among the shards of the failed dream, our children will have to try to build their lives...

But now, let's turn our attention from failures & threats to successes. Today, thousands of airliners successfully took to the skies, because they were designed in harmony with the laws of aerodynamics & strength of materials. America has successfully produced the happiness & prosperity of unprecedented millions because it was designed in harmony with the laws of nature & nature's God. These laws are not optional, nor negotiable. Applying political will to these laws is like building an airliner out of cast iron -- it just won't fly. This is why Wal-Mart stores were not the result of a government program & McDonald's restaurants were not a bureaucracy's brainchild. These institutions came from individuals, in small groups, who took good ideas, added hard work & persistence & created success. Collectivists despise them, not because they are bad, but because do not need Collectivist patronage. It was not simply a happy accident that the automobile, the primary mode of transportation of the 20th century, was not created by the owners of the dominant transportation modes of the 19th century -- trains, ships & horses. Nor was it just a coincidence that the stunning advances in aerospace technology in the 20th century came out of air races & prizes, & places like Lockheed's Skunkworks, that operated outside of the culture of the man in the gray flannel suit. Nor was it chance that the personal computer revolution was sparked by two guys in an old apple orchard & a college dropout. Ashby's & Livingston's Laws show that what changes the game is when innovators have the liberty to operate beyond the boundaries of official approval.

> **We can't afford to cower down, hoping that a stone from the sky won't knock us back to the Stone Age.**

When it comes to major crises, Hollywood movies have humanity mounting an effort to divert such the catastrophe in a span of weeks or months. This is not going to happen. The infrastructure required would take decades to build. It would be as if we accosted the Framers of the Constitution leaving Independence Hall in 1787 & challenged them with this: "America is going to need a road network for millions of horseless carriages that will let anyone travel across this continent, at speeds of a mile a minute." Even the redoubtable Ben Franklin would despair at the prospect. They certainly couldn't conceive of doing it in weeks, or months, or even years. And yet, America would do that. It took a century & a half, but -- we did that. And we can prepare to cope with, or prevent, real global threats, like catastrophic meteor strikes. But not in a sudden, centralized, movie-style effort. "Live free or die!" isn't a

copyright © 2016 J. M. Payne

slogan for selfish rebels; it is a survival strategy. To cope with the future we have to be free innovate, adapt & iterate our solutions. We can't afford to cower down, hoping that a stone falling from the sky won't knock us back to the Stone Age, or that an EMP event will put out the lights of civilization. We have a fighting chance -- if we have the vision & the freedom to fight.

But our vision for freedom has been dimmed by living so long in the shadows of a government dominated society. Frederick Douglass reported a similar effect after his escape from slavery, in his "Narrative":

> "I had very strangely supposed, while in slavery, that few of the comforts, & scarcely any of the luxuries, of life were enjoyed at the north, compared with what were enjoyed by the slaveholders of the south. I supposed that they were about upon a level with the non-slaveholding population of the south. I knew they were exceedingly poor, & I had been accustomed to regard their poverty as the necessary consequence of their being non-slaveholders. I had somehow imbibed the opinion that, in the absence of slaves, there could be no wealth, & very little refinement. And upon coming to the north, I expected to meet with a rough, hard-handed & uncultivated population, living in the most Spartan-like simplicity, knowing nothing of the ease, luxury, pomp & grandeur of southern slaveholders."

Today, we have much the same feeling about absence of the nanny-state that Mr. Douglass had about the absence of slavery -- we cannot imagine a society working properly otherwise. The myth of the nanny-state is to presume that, since scientists & engineers are adept at manipulating things, then politicians are adept at manipulating people. Human problems are far more complex & dynamic than that. So, I offer no "14-point agenda" or "5 easy steps" to quickly & easily set everything right, & you should not trust it, if I did. In a nation of over 300 million people, each of us has a good idea about something; I hope that some of the ideas herein are worth implementing. But the nature of a free society is that we cannot know the end from beginning; improvisation is indispensable for a free people.

The objection will be raised that this amounts to the abolition of government & the embrace of anarchy. To which we can reply, "Just because we don't want government to do everything, does not mean we don't want it to do anything." Yet, if government is not be our shepherd, then who? What will keep us from the chaos of each doing what is right in our own eyes, if we are not bound the rules & procedures that now permeate our lives? Unity created by authority is limited by fear; unity

copyright 2016 © J. M. Payne

arising from humility is powered by faith. We must be humble enough to recover the faith that our story is being written by a Divine Author, that we must fit into His narrative. As Abraham Lincoln put it, "We have forgotten God. We have forgotten the gracious hand which preserved us in peace and multiplied & enriched & strengthened us, & we have vainly imagined in the deceitfulness of our hearts that all these blessings were produced by some superior wisdom & virtue of our own. Intoxicated with unbroken success, we have become too self-sufficient to feel the necessity of redeeming & preserving grace – too proud to pray to the God that made us." But humbled under His hand, we are freed to weave our stories into His larger one. This liberty allows us to learn from our failures, because denying failure prevents learning. When truths earned through hard experience are accepted, our mental models can be improved. Instead of blindly following the dictates of authority, the creative power of the whole society is engaged. This is how the fabric of human society best supports the strain of complex challenges.

Both blue jeans & cheese cloth are made from cotton thread. Jeans are famous for being functional & durable. But jeans made from cheesecloth would provide little protection or privacy when new & would rapidly worsen. Soon they would be little more than a trail of threads behind their former wearer. Denim is more durable than cheesecloth, because of the threads' connections. Denim is tightly woven, so each thread shares the load with others. Gaps are tiny, so it's hard for anything to snag the fabric. Society's fabric is made of the threads of relationships. Our communities used to be tightly woven, like denim, but over time they have loosened until they're more like cheesecloth. We unraveled our society & called it progress. Mothers, children, fathers, singles, the elderly are exposed to the snags of life. Instead of sharing our burdens, we relied on bureaucracies. And the politicians, no matter how many laws they write or how much money they spend, can't build bureaucracies fast enough to replace the organic relationships being displaced. So society is riddled with gaps, & people are falling through those gaps. We must learn to weave our society together again, to repair the unraveling that's been done in our rush to progress.

Going forward, we will need even more freedom to imagine & create the tapestry of innovations & relationships needed to meet the coming challenges. We are still in the dawn of the Information Revolution. It can be an era of innovation as vast & consequential as the Agricultural or Industrial Revolutions. For the 1st time in human history, we could live in a world where everybody is rich, not just those in the "advanced" nations. What is really at stake now is everybody's future; perhaps everybody's survival. I have hope that we can survive, & survive with style. That phase comes from Jerry Pournelle's visionary book, "A Step

copyright © 2016 J. M. Payne

Farther Out". It outlines a strategy for a future, not of diminished expectations, but of dazzling possibilities. It was written back in 1979, but his analyses of technical & social trends have held up rather well:

- ☐ That the next step in the computer revolution would be direct neural interface to the brain. Prosthetic hands are now being neurally controlled & work is being done to add a sense of touch to these devices.

- ☐ That a population bust, not boom, would be humanity's real problem. We are seeing this in the demographic pressures that are bankrupting retirement programs & changing cultures around the world.

- ☐ That there should be a renaissance in nuclear power, because the numbers say that "green" energy simply can't fulfill humanity's needs. That renaissance is happening, though with some significant setbacks.

- ☐ That OTEC - ocean thermal energy conversion - is a viable, non-polluting energy technology. Lockheed Martin recently signed a contract to design a 10-megawatt OTEC power plant – the world's largest to date.

- ☐ That getting to LEO - low earth orbit - gets us half way to anywhere & is the 1st step in building the infrastructure to open up vast new sources of energy & materials (& avoid a catastrophic impact event). Though today, the only way for an American to reach space is to hitch a ride on someone else's rocket, NASA's Orion & SpaceX's Falcon 9 spacecraft promise to soon end this shameful episode in American technological history.

Most significantly, barriers to individual innovation & production are being erased. We have the technology to get into space & recent discoveries give us a new reason to believe we can stay there: water has been discovered on our Moon. Aside from being necessary to sustaining life, water is made of of hydrogen & oxygen -- which is rocket fuel. It is estimated there could be 660 million tons of ice in permanently shadowed areas near the moon's north pole. Evidence of water has also been detected at the Moon's south pole. Ongoing advances in robotics make building the infrastructure needed for us to get up there more viable than ever before. We no longer need 20th century-style corporate or government mega-organization to do big things. Whatever an innovator imagines can be built using in plastic, metal, or even biological materials, by 3D printers & machining centers that can cost less than a used car. Or the inventor can send his 3D computer model to vendors anywhere in the world to build what he needs in a variety of

copyright 2016 © J. M. Payne

materials at affordable prices. And these inventors can run through multiple cycles of innovation in the time that a centralized bureaucracy needed just to request a proposal. That system's means of financing & distribution are also being superseded through the internet revolution. The old system - the one that Collectivism wants to protect & expand - is just not capable of realizing this future.

Perhaps more importantly, the people running that system don't _want_ this future. A future of innovation will be one in which the status quo is in continual upheaval. This means that the Better Sort of people will not be able to stay at the top. History says that those on top are quite willing for the rest of us live in poverty, as long as they get to stay on top. And, chillingly, this round of the struggle may be the last. As Pournelle puts it, "... ours may be the only century in all of history when Mankind can break free of earth. Our opportunity may not come again, per omnia seculae seculorum. ... There are no end of foreseeable crises, & enough of them could so deplete our resource base & technological ability that when we realize that we _must_ go into space, we won't be able to get there." We can let that happen to us & our posterity. Or we can leave our children the legacy of a world of wealth & a pathway to the stars.

> **"If men are to remain civilized or to become so, the art of associating together must grow & improve in the same ratio in which the equality of conditions is increased" -- Alexis de Tocqueville**

Speaking of children, it has become very popular to claim that America's kids are not up to the challenge of this future. The conventional response to this is to blame society & pour more authority & funding to the same systems that produced the failure. We should reject both the slander against us & the blind faith in bureaucracy. School bureaucracies teach, by example if not curriculum, that obedience is better than innovation; that participation is better than competition; that fear is better than faith. Even something as wholesome as school recess has been removed as being too risky. How can our kids compete with the world, when we don't even allow them to compete with each other? But not all trends are towards turning children into sheep. Homeschooling is liberating an increasing number of children from these chains & reintegrating education into all of life & community. And, technical competitions are becoming more popular, like US FIRST robotics. It has some 44,000 teams involving 400,000 students from elementary through high school. These kids aren't just building robots; they're learning how to work in teams to solve problems, & how to work the run-break-fix cycle to prove that their

copyright © 2016 J. M. Payne

solutions work.   And, FIRST's values of Gracious Professionalism® & Coopertition® teach the children to behave with grace & honor even while fiercely competing. These kids work as hard as on their robots as any high school football team practices for their games. FIRST did not spring from a government initiative; it came from the mind of entrepreneur Dean Kamen. His vision is, "To transform our culture by creating a world where science and technology are celebrated and where young people dream of becoming science and technology leaders." The kids in FIRST are building, for practice, for competition, & for fun, machines that, when I was born, existed only in science fiction. This should not surprise us. Today, kids use smart phones that would put the communicator of Star Trek's Captain Kirk to shame, & they do it with ease. These kids are the future -- or they can be. The question is, will this fertile creativity end with these competitions? Will they then be forced to accept "...that small measure of an American Dream," that politicians think is all they deserve?

I submit that the answer depends on whether we apply Livingston's & Ashby's Laws to tame our control infrastructure & redevelop our social infrastructure, so that we are freed to take advantage of the emerging opportunities. In terms of the Liberty vs. Complexity diagram above, if we're going to get to where the coping line remains above the chaos line, that is, in the region of Liberty, people must again become very adept at the art of associating together. This was well understood in America, over a century ago. Again, quoting de Tocqueville: "Among the laws that rule human societies there is one which seems to be more precise & clear than all others. If men are to remain civilized or to become so, the art of associating together must grow & improve in the same ratio in which the equality of conditions is increased". Nothing that we need to do to repair society is really new. As King Solomon told us in the 1st chapter of Ecclesiastes, "...there is nothing new under the sun. Is there anything of which it may be said, 'See, this is new'? It has already been in ancient times before us." We have done this before, in the Great Awakenings, & after the Revolutionary & Civil Wars. We simply have to remember, believe & act. This is how the children of the 21st century can have the freedom to create the kinds of expanded opportunities that those of the 20th century saw.

Can we do this? Yes, we can.

copyright 2016 © J. M. Payne

VI. APPENDIX:

THE DECLARATION OF INDEPENDENCE:

When in the Course of human events, it becomes necessary for one people to dissolve the political bands which have connected them with another, and to assume among the powers of the earth, the separate and equal station to which the Laws of Nature and of Nature's God entitle them, a decent respect to the opinions of mankind requires that they should declare the causes which impel them to the separation.

We hold these truths to be self-evident, that all men are created equal, that they are endowed by their Creator with certain unalienable Rights, that among these are Life, Liberty and the pursuit of Happiness.--That to secure these rights, Governments are instituted among Men, deriving their just powers from the consent of the governed, --That whenever any Form of Government becomes destructive of these ends, it is the Right of the People to alter or to abolish it, and to institute new Government, laying its foundation on such principles and organizing its powers in such form, as to them shall seem most likely to effect their Safety and Happiness. Prudence, indeed, will dictate that Governments long established should not be changed for light and transient causes; and accordingly all experience hath shewn, that mankind are more disposed to suffer, while evils are sufferable, than to right themselves by abolishing the forms to which they are accustomed. But when a long train of abuses and usurpations, pursuing invariably the same Object evinces a design to reduce them under absolute Despotism, it is their right, it is their duty, to throw off such Government, and to provide new Guards for their future security.--Such has been the patient sufferance of these Colonies; and such is now the necessity which constrains them to alter their former Systems of Government. The history of the present King of Great Britain is a history of repeated injuries and usurpations, all having in direct object the establishment of an absolute Tyranny over these States. To prove this, let Facts be submitted to a candid world.

(1) He has refused his Assent to Laws, the most wholesome and necessary for the public good.

(2) He has forbidden his Governors to pass Laws of immediate and pressing importance, unless suspended in their operation till his Assent should be obtained; and when so suspended, he has utterly neglected to attend to them.

copyright © 2016 J. M. Payne

(3) He has refused to pass other Laws for the accommodation of large districts of people, unless those people would relinquish the right of Representation in the Legislature, a right inestimable to them and formidable to tyrants only.

(4) He has called together legislative bodies at places unusual, uncomfortable, and distant from the depository of their public Records, for the sole purpose of fatiguing them into compliance with his measures.

(5) He has dissolved Representative Houses repeatedly, for opposing with manly firmness his invasions on the rights of the people.

(6) He has refused for a long time, after such dissolutions, to cause others to be elected; whereby the Legislative powers, incapable of Annihilation, have returned to the People at large for their exercise; the State remaining in the mean time exposed to all the dangers of invasion from without, and convulsions within.

(7) He has endeavoured to prevent the population of these States; for that purpose obstructing the Laws for Naturalization of Foreigners; refusing to pass others to encourage their migrations hither, and raising the conditions of new Appropriations of Lands.

(8) He has obstructed the Administration of Justice, by refusing his Assent to Laws for establishing Judiciary powers.

(9) He has made Judges dependent on his Will alone, for the tenure of their offices, and the amount and payment of their salaries.

(10) He has erected a multitude of New Offices, and sent hither swarms of Officers to harrass our people, and eat out their substance.

(11) He has kept among us, in times of peace, Standing Armies without the Consent of our legislatures.

(12) He has affected to render the Military independent of and superior to the Civil power.

(13) He has combined with others to subject us to a jurisdiction foreign to our constitution, and unacknowledged by our laws; giving his Assent to their Acts of pretended Legislation:
For Quartering large bodies of armed troops among us:
For protecting them, by a mock Trial, from punishment for any Murders which they should commit on the Inhabitants of these States:
For cutting off our Trade with all parts of the world:
For imposing Taxes on us without our Consent:
For depriving us in many cases, of the benefits of Trial by Jury:

copyright 2016 © J. M. Payne

For transporting us beyond Seas to be tried for pretended offences
For abolishing the free System of English Laws in a neighbouring
Province, establishing therein an Arbitrary government, and
enlarging its Boundaries so as to render it at once an example and
fit instrument for introducing the same absolute rule into these
Colonies:
For taking away our Charters, abolishing our most valuable Laws,
and altering fundamentally the Forms of our Governments:
For suspending our own Legislatures, and declaring themselves
invested with power to legislate for us in all cases whatsoever.

(14) He has abdicated Government here, by declaring us out of his
Protection and waging War against us.

(15) He has plundered our seas, ravaged our Coasts, burnt our towns,
and destroyed the lives of our people.

(16) He is at this time transporting large Armies of foreign Mercenaries
to compleat the works of death, desolation and tyranny, already
begun with circumstances of Cruelty & perfidy scarcely paralleled
in the most barbarous ages, and totally unworthy the Head of a
civilized nation.

(17) He has constrained our fellow Citizens taken Captive on the high
Seas to bear Arms against their Country, to become the
executioners of their friends and Brethren, or to fall themselves by
their Hands.

(18) He has excited domestic insurrections amongst us, and has
endeavoured to bring on the inhabitants of our frontiers, the
merciless Indian Savages, whose known rule of warfare, is an
undistinguished destruction of all ages, sexes and conditions.

In every stage of these Oppressions We have Petitioned for Redress in
the most humble terms: Our repeated Petitions have been answered
only by repeated injury. A Prince whose character is thus marked by
every act which may define a Tyrant, is unfit to be the ruler of a free
people.

Nor have We been wanting in attentions to our Brittish brethren. We
have warned them from time to time of attempts by their legislature to
extend an unwarrantable jurisdiction over us. We have reminded them
of the circumstances of our emigration and settlement here. We have
appealed to their native justice and magnanimity, and we have conjured
them by the ties of our common kindred to disavow these usurpations,
which, would inevitably interrupt our connections and correspondence.
They too have been deaf to the voice of justice and of consanguinity. We
must, therefore, acquiesce in the necessity, which denounces our

copyright © 2016 J. M. Payne

Separation, and hold them, as we hold the rest of mankind, Enemies in War, in Peace Friends.

We, therefore, the Representatives of the united States of America, in General Congress, Assembled, appealing to the Supreme Judge of the world for the rectitude of our intentions, do, in the Name, and by Authority of the good People of these Colonies, solemnly publish and declare, That these United Colonies are, and of Right ought to be Free and Independent States; that they are Absolved from all Allegiance to the British Crown, and that all political connection between them and the State of Great Britain, is and ought to be totally dissolved; and that as Free and Independent States, they have full Power to levy War, conclude Peace, contract Alliances, establish Commerce, and to do all other Acts and Things which Independent States may of right do. And for the support of this Declaration, with a firm reliance on the protection of divine Providence, we mutually pledge to each other our Lives, our Fortunes and our sacred Honor.

Georgia:
  Button Gwinnett
  Lyman Hall
  George Walton

North Carolina:
  William Hooper
  Joseph Hewes
  John Penn
South Carolina:
  Edward Rutledge
  Thomas Heyward, Jr.
  Thomas Lynch, Jr.
  Arthur Middleton

Massachusetts:
John Hancock
Maryland:
Samuel Chase
William Paca
Thomas Stone
Charles Carroll of Carrollton
Virginia:
George Wythe
Richard Henry Lee
Thomas Jefferson
Benjamin Harrison
Thomas Nelson, Jr.
Francis Lightfoot Lee
Carter Braxton

copyright 2016 © J. M. Payne

Pennsylvania:
  Robert Morris
  Benjamin Rush
  Benjamin Franklin
  John Morton
  George Clymer
  James Smith
  George Taylor
  James Wilson
  George Ross
Delaware:
  Caesar Rodney
  George Read
  Thomas McKean

New York:
  William Floyd
  Philip Livingston
  Francis Lewis
  Lewis Morris
New Jersey:
  Richard Stockton
  John Witherspoon
  Francis
Hopkinson
  John Hart
  Abraham Clark

New Hampshire:
  Josiah Bartlett
  William Whipple
Massachusetts:
  Samuel Adams
  John Adams
  Robert Treat
Paine
  Elbridge Gerry
Rhode Island:
  Stephen Hopkins
  William Ellery
Connecticut:
  Roger Sherman
  Samuel
Huntington
  William Williams
  Oliver Wolcott
New Hampshire:
  Matthew
Thornton

copyright © 2016 J. M. Payne

THE CONSTITUTION OF THE UNITED STATES:

(Underlined text superseded by amendment)

LETTER OF TRANSMITTAL TO CONGRESS:

IN CONVENTION MONDAY SEPTEMBER 17th 1787.

Present

The States of

New Hampshire, Massachusetts, Connecticut, Mr. Hamilton from New York, New Jersey, Pennsylvania, Delaware, Maryland, Virginia, North Carolina, South Carolina and Georgia. Resolved,

That the proceeding Constitution be laid before the United States in Congress assembled, and that it is the Opinion of this Convention, that it should afterwards be submitted to a Convention of Delegates, chosen in each State by the People thereof, under the Recommendation of its Legislature, for their Assent and Ratification; and that each Convention assenting to, and ratifying the Same, should give Notice thereof to the United States in Congress assembled.

Resolved, That it is the Opinion of this Convention, that as soon as the Conventions of nine States shall have ratified this Constitution, the United States in Congress assembled should fix a Day on which Electors should be appointed by the States which shall have ratified the same, and a Day on which the Electors should assemble to vote for the President, and the Time and Place for commencing Proceedings under this Constitution. That after such Publication the Electors should be appointed, and the Senators and Representatives elected: That the Electors should meet on the Day fixed for the Election of the President, and should transmit their Votes certified, signed, sealed and directed, as the Constitution requires, to the Secretary of the United States in Congress assembled, that the Senators and Representatives should convene at the Time and Place assigned; that the Senators should appoint a President of the Senate, for the sole Purpose of receiving, opening and counting the Votes for President; and, that after he shall be chosen, the Congress, together with the President, should, without Delay, proceed to execute this Constitution.

By the Unanimous Order of the Convention

Go WASHINGTON Presidt

W. JACKSON Secretary.

copyright 2016 © J. M. Payne

RESOLUTION OF CONGRESS OF SEPTEMBER 28, 1787, SUBMITTING THE CONSTITUTION TO THE SEVERAL STATES:

Friday Sept. 28. 1787

Congress assembled present New Hampshire Massachusetts Connecticut New York New Jersey Pennsylvania. Delaware Virginia North Carolina South Carolina and Georgia and from Maryland Mr Ross

Congress having received the report of the Convention lately assembled in Philadelphia

Resolved Unanimously that the said Report with the resolutions and letter accompanying the same be transmitted to the several legislatures in Order to be submitted to a convention of Delegates chosen in each state by the people thereof in conformity to the resolves of the Convention made and provided in that case.

We the People of the United States, in Order to form a more perfect Union, establish Justice, insure domestic Tranquility, provide for the common defence, promote the general Welfare, and secure the Blessings of Liberty to ourselves and our Posterity, do ordain and establish this Constitution for the United States of America.

Article. I.

Section. 1.

All legislative Powers herein granted shall be vested in a Congress of the United States, which shall consist of a Senate and House of Representatives.

Section. 2.

The House of Representatives shall be composed of Members chosen every second Year by the People of the several States, and the Electors in each State shall have the Qualifications requisite for Electors of the most numerous Branch of the State Legislature.

No Person shall be a Representative who shall not have attained to the Age of twenty five Years, and been seven Years a Citizen of the United States, and who shall not, when elected, be an Inhabitant of that State in which he shall be chosen.

Representatives and direct Taxes shall be apportioned among the several States which may be included within this Union, according to

copyright © 2016 J. M. Payne

their respective Numbers, which shall be determined by adding to the whole Number of free Persons, including those bound to Service for a Term of Years, and excluding Indians not taxed, three fifths of all other Persons. The actual Enumeration shall be made within three Years after the first Meeting of the Congress of the United States, and within every subsequent Term of ten Years, in such Manner as they shall by Law direct. The Number of Representatives shall not exceed one for every thirty Thousand, but each State shall have at Least one Representative; and until such enumeration shall be made, the State of New Hampshire shall be entitled to chuse three, Massachusetts eight, Rhode-Island and Providence Plantations one, Connecticut five, New-York six, New Jersey four, Pennsylvania eight, Delaware one, Maryland six, Virginia ten, North Carolina five, South Carolina five, and Georgia three.

When vacancies happen in the Representation from any State, the Executive Authority thereof shall issue Writs of Election to fill such Vacancies.

The House of Representatives shall chuse their Speaker and other Officers; and shall have the sole Power of Impeachment.

Section. 3.

The Senate of the United States shall be composed of two Senators from each State, chosen by the Legislature thereof for six Years; and each Senator shall have one Vote.

Immediately after they shall be assembled in Consequence of the first Election, they shall be divided as equally as may be into three Classes. The Seats of the Senators of the first Class shall be vacated at the Expiration of the second Year, of the second Class at the Expiration of the fourth Year, and of the third Class at the Expiration of the sixth Year, so that one third may be chosen every second Year; and if Vacancies happen by Resignation, or otherwise, during the Recess of the Legislature of any State, the Executive thereof may make temporary Appointments until the next Meeting of the Legislature, which shall then fill such Vacancies.

No Person shall be a Senator who shall not have attained to the Age of thirty Years, and been nine Years a Citizen of the United States, and who shall not, when elected, be an Inhabitant of that State for which he shall be chosen.

The Vice President of the United States shall be President of the Senate, but shall have no Vote, unless they be equally divided.

copyright 2016 © J. M. Payne

The Senate shall chuse their other Officers, and also a President pro tempore, in the Absence of the Vice President, or when he shall exercise the Office of President of the United States.

The Senate shall have the sole Power to try all Impeachments. When sitting for that Purpose, they shall be on Oath or Affirmation. When the President of the United States is tried, the Chief Justice shall preside: And no Person shall be convicted without the Concurrence of two thirds of the Members present.

Judgment in Cases of Impeachment shall not extend further than to removal from Office, and disqualification to hold and enjoy any Office of honor, Trust or Profit under the United States: but the Party convicted shall nevertheless be liable and subject to Indictment, Trial, Judgment and Punishment, according to Law.

Section. 4.

The Times, Places and Manner of holding Elections for Senators and Representatives, shall be prescribed in each State by the Legislature thereof; but the Congress may at any time by Law make or alter such Regulations, except as to the Places of chusing Senators.

The Congress shall assemble at least once in every Year, and such Meeting shall be on the first Monday in December, unless they shall by Law appoint a different Day.

Section. 5.

Each House shall be the Judge of the Elections, Returns and Qualifications of its own Members, and a Majority of each shall constitute a Quorum to do Business; but a smaller Number may adjourn from day to day, and may be authorized to compel the Attendance of absent Members, in such Manner, and under such Penalties as each House may provide.

Each House may determine the Rules of its Proceedings, punish its Members for disorderly Behaviour, and, with the Concurrence of two thirds, expel a Member.

Each House shall keep a Journal of its Proceedings, and from time to time publish the same, excepting such Parts as may in their Judgment require Secrecy; and the Yeas and Nays of the Members of either House on any question shall, at the Desire of one fifth of those Present, be entered on the Journal.

Neither House, during the Session of Congress, shall, without the Consent of the other, adjourn for more than three days, nor to any other Place than that in which the two Houses shall be sitting.

copyright © 2016 J. M. Payne

Section. 6.

The Senators and Representatives shall receive a Compensation for their Services, to be ascertained by Law, and paid out of the Treasury of the United States. They shall in all Cases, except Treason, Felony and Breach of the Peace, be privileged from Arrest during their Attendance at the Session of their respective Houses, and in going to and returning from the same; and for any Speech or Debate in either House, they shall not be questioned in any other Place.

No Senator or Representative shall, during the Time for which he was elected, be appointed to any civil Office under the Authority of the United States, which shall have been created, or the Emoluments whereof shall have been encreased during such time; and no Person holding any Office under the United States, shall be a Member of either House during his Continuance in Office.

Section. 7.

All Bills for raising Revenue shall originate in the House of Representatives; but the Senate may propose or concur with Amendments as on other Bills.

Every Bill which shall have passed the House of Representatives and the Senate, shall, before it become a Law, be presented to the President of the United States: If he approve he shall sign it, but if not he shall return it, with his Objections to that House in which it shall have originated, who shall enter the Objections at large on their Journal, and proceed to reconsider it. If after such Reconsideration two thirds of that House shall agree to pass the Bill, it shall be sent, together with the Objections, to the other House, by which it shall likewise be reconsidered, and if approved by two thirds of that House, it shall become a Law. But in all such Cases the Votes of both Houses shall be determined by yeas and Nays, and the Names of the Persons voting for and against the Bill shall be entered on the Journal of each House respectively. If any Bill shall not be returned by the President within ten Days (Sundays excepted) after it shall have been presented to him, the Same shall be a Law, in like Manner as if he had signed it, unless the Congress by their Adjournment prevent its Return, in which Case it shall not be a Law.

Every Order, Resolution, or Vote to which the Concurrence of the Senate and House of Representatives may be necessary (except on a question of Adjournment) shall be presented to the President of the United States; and before the Same shall take Effect, shall be approved by him, or being disapproved by him, shall be repassed by two thirds of the

copyright 2016 © J. M. Payne

Senate and House of Representatives, according to the Rules and Limitations prescribed in the Case of a Bill.

Section. 8.

The Congress shall have Power

(1) To lay and collect Taxes, Duties, Imposts and Excises, to pay the Debts and provide for the common Defence and general Welfare of the United States; but all Duties, Imposts and Excises shall be uniform throughout the United States;

(2) To borrow Money on the credit of the United States;

(3) To regulate Commerce with foreign Nations, and among the several States, and with the Indian Tribes;

(4) To establish an uniform Rule of Naturalization, and uniform Laws on the subject of Bankruptcies throughout the United States;

(5) To coin Money, regulate the Value thereof, and of foreign Coin, and fix the Standard of Weights and Measures;

(6) To provide for the Punishment of counterfeiting the Securities and current Coin of the United States;

(7) To establish Post Offices and post Roads;

(8) To promote the Progress of Science and useful Arts, by securing for limited Times to Authors and Inventors the exclusive Right to their respective Writings and Discoveries;

(9) To constitute Tribunals inferior to the supreme Court;

(10) To define and punish Piracies and Felonies committed on the high Seas, and Offences against the Law of Nations;

(11) To declare War, grant Letters of Marque and Reprisal, and make Rules concerning Captures on Land and Water;

(12) To raise and support Armies, but no Appropriation of Money to that Use shall be for a longer Term than two Years;

(13) To provide and maintain a Navy;

(14) To make Rules for the Government and Regulation of the land and naval Forces;

(15) To provide for calling forth the Militia to execute the Laws of the Union, suppress Insurrections and repel Invasions;

copyright © 2016 J. M. Payne

(16) To provide for organizing, arming, and disciplining, the Militia, and for governing such Part of them as may be employed in the Service of the United States, reserving to the States respectively, the Appointment of the Officers, and the Authority of training the Militia according to the discipline prescribed by Congress;

(17) To exercise exclusive Legislation in all Cases whatsoever, over such District (not exceeding ten Miles square) as may, by Cession of particular States, and the Acceptance of Congress, become the Seat of the Government of the United States, and to exercise like Authority over all Places purchased by the Consent of the Legislature of the State in which the Same shall be, for the Erection of Forts, Magazines, Arsenals, dock-Yards, and other needful Buildings;--And

(18) To make all Laws which shall be necessary and proper for carrying into Execution the foregoing Powers, and all other Powers vested by this Constitution in the Government of the United States, or in any Department or Officer thereof.

Section. 9.

The Migration or Importation of such Persons as any of the States now existing shall think proper to admit, shall not be prohibited by the Congress prior to the Year one thousand eight hundred and eight, but a Tax or duty may be imposed on such Importation, not exceeding ten dollars for each Person.

The Privilege of the Writ of Habeas Corpus shall not be suspended, unless when in Cases of Rebellion or Invasion the public Safety may require it.

No Bill of Attainder or ex post facto Law shall be passed.

No Capitation, or other direct, Tax shall be laid, <u>unless in Proportion to the Census or enumeration herein before directed to be taken</u>.

No Tax or Duty shall be laid on Articles exported from any State.

No Preference shall be given by any Regulation of Commerce or Revenue to the Ports of one State over those of another; nor shall Vessels bound to, or from, one State, be obliged to enter, clear, or pay Duties in another.

No Money shall be drawn from the Treasury, but in Consequence of Appropriations made by Law; and a regular Statement and Account of the Receipts and Expenditures of all public Money shall be published from time to time.

copyright 2016 © J. M. Payne

No Title of Nobility shall be granted by the United States: And no Person holding any Office of Profit or Trust under them, shall, without the Consent of the Congress, accept of any present, Emolument, Office, or Title, of any kind whatever, from any King, Prince, or foreign State.

Section. 10.

No State shall enter into any Treaty, Alliance, or Confederation; grant Letters of Marque and Reprisal; coin Money; emit Bills of Credit; make any Thing but gold and silver Coin a Tender in Payment of Debts; pass any Bill of Attainder, ex post facto Law, or Law impairing the Obligation of Contracts, or grant any Title of Nobility.

No State shall, without the Consent of the Congress, lay any Imposts or Duties on Imports or Exports, except what may be absolutely necessary for executing it's inspection Laws: and the net Produce of all Duties and Imposts, laid by any State on Imports or Exports, shall be for the Use of the Treasury of the United States; and all such Laws shall be subject to the Revision and Controul of the Congress.

No State shall, without the Consent of Congress, lay any Duty of Tonnage, keep Troops, or Ships of War in time of Peace, enter into any Agreement or Compact with another State, or with a foreign Power, or engage in War, unless actually invaded, or in such imminent Danger as will not admit of delay.

Article. II.

Section. 1.

The executive Power shall be vested in a President of the United States of America. He shall hold his Office during the Term of four Years, and, together with the Vice President, chosen for the same Term, be elected, as follows:

Each State shall appoint, in such Manner as the Legislature thereof may direct, a Number of Electors, equal to the whole Number of Senators and Representatives to which the State may be entitled in the Congress: but no Senator or Representative, or Person holding an Office of Trust or Profit under the United States, shall be appointed an Elector.

The Electors shall meet in their respective States, and vote by Ballot for two Persons, of whom one at least shall not be an Inhabitant of the same State with themselves. And they shall make a List of all the Persons voted for, and of the Number of Votes for each; which List they shall sign and certify, and transmit sealed to the Seat of the Government of the United States, directed to the President of the Senate. The President of the Senate shall, in the Presence of the Senate and House of Representatives, open all the Certificates, and the Votes shall then be

copyright © 2016 J. M. Payne

counted. The Person having the greatest Number of Votes shall be the President, if such Number be a Majority of the whole Number of Electors appointed; and if there be more than one who have such Majority, and have an equal Number of Votes, then the House of Representatives shall immediately chuse by Ballot one of them for President; and if no Person have a Majority, then from the five highest on the List the said House shall in like Manner chuse the President. But in chusing the President, the Votes shall be taken by States, the Representation from each State having one Vote; A quorum for this purpose shall consist of a Member or Members from two thirds of the States, and a Majority of all the States shall be necessary to a Choice. In every Case, after the Choice of the President, the Person having the greatest Number of Votes of the Electors shall be the Vice President. But if there should remain two or more who have equal Votes, the Senate shall chuse from them by Ballot the Vice President.

The Congress may determine the Time of chusing the Electors, and the Day on which they shall give their Votes; which Day shall be the same throughout the United States.

No Person except a natural born Citizen, or a Citizen of the United States, at the time of the Adoption of this Constitution, shall be eligible to the Office of President; neither shall any Person be eligible to that Office who shall not have attained to the Age of thirty five Years, and been fourteen Years a Resident within the United States.

In Case of the Removal of the President from Office, or of his Death, Resignation, or Inability to discharge the Powers and Duties of the said Office, the Same shall devolve on the Vice President, and the Congress may by Law provide for the Case of Removal, Death, Resignation or Inability, both of the President and Vice President, declaring what Officer shall then act as President, and such Officer shall act accordingly, until the Disability be removed, or a President shall be elected.

The President shall, at stated Times, receive for his Services, a Compensation, which shall neither be increased nor diminished during the Period for which he shall have been elected, and he shall not receive within that Period any other Emolument from the United States, or any of them.

Before he enter on the Execution of his Office, he shall take the following Oath or Affirmation:--"I do solemnly swear (or affirm) that I will faithfully execute the Office of President of the United States, and will to the best of my Ability, preserve, protect and defend the Constitution of the United States."

copyright 2016 © J. M. Payne

Section. 2.

The President shall be Commander in Chief of the Army and Navy of the United States, and of the Militia of the several States, when called into the actual Service of the United States; he may require the Opinion, in writing, of the principal Officer in each of the executive Departments, upon any Subject relating to the Duties of their respective Offices, and he shall have Power to grant Reprieves and Pardons for Offences against the United States, except in Cases of Impeachment.

He shall have Power, by and with the Advice and Consent of the Senate, to make Treaties, provided two thirds of the Senators present concur; and he shall nominate, and by and with the Advice and Consent of the Senate, shall appoint Ambassadors, other public Ministers and Consuls, Judges of the supreme Court, and all other Officers of the United States, whose Appointments are not herein otherwise provided for, and which shall be established by Law: but the Congress may by Law vest the Appointment of such inferior Officers, as they think proper, in the President alone, in the Courts of Law, or in the Heads of Departments.

The President shall have Power to fill up all Vacancies that may happen during the Recess of the Senate, by granting Commissions which shall expire at the End of their next Session.

Section. 3.

He shall from time to time give to the Congress Information of the State of the Union, and recommend to their Consideration such Measures as he shall judge necessary and expedient; he may, on extraordinary Occasions, convene both Houses, or either of them, and in Case of Disagreement between them, with Respect to the Time of Adjournment, he may adjourn them to such Time as he shall think proper; he shall receive Ambassadors and other public Ministers; he shall take Care that the Laws be faithfully executed, and shall Commission all the Officers of the United States.

Section. 4.

The President, Vice President and all civil Officers of the United States, shall be removed from Office on Impeachment for, and Conviction of, Treason, Bribery, or other high Crimes and Misdemeanors.

Article III.

Section. 1.

The judicial Power of the United States shall be vested in one supreme Court, and in such inferior Courts as the Congress may from time to time ordain and establish. The Judges, both of the supreme and inferior

copyright © 2016 J. M. Payne

Courts, shall hold their Offices during good Behaviour, and shall, at stated Times, receive for their Services a Compensation, which shall not be diminished during their Continuance in Office.

Section. 2.

The judicial Power shall extend to all Cases, in Law and Equity, arising under this Constitution, the Laws of the United States, and Treaties made, or which shall be made, under their Authority;--to all Cases affecting Ambassadors, other public Ministers and Consuls;--to all Cases of admiralty and maritime Jurisdiction;--to Controversies to which the United States shall be a Party;--to Controversies between two or more States;-- between a State and Citizens of another State,--between Citizens of different States,--between Citizens of the same State claiming Lands under Grants of different States, and between a State, or the Citizens thereof, and foreign States, Citizens or Subjects.

In all Cases affecting Ambassadors, other public Ministers and Consuls, and those in which a State shall be Party, the supreme Court shall have original Jurisdiction. In all the other Cases before mentioned, the supreme Court shall have appellate Jurisdiction, both as to Law and Fact, with such Exceptions, and under such Regulations as the Congress shall make.

The Trial of all Crimes, except in Cases of Impeachment, shall be by Jury; and such Trial shall be held in the State where the said Crimes shall have been committed; but when not committed within any State, the Trial shall be at such Place or Places as the Congress may by Law have directed.

Section. 3.

Treason against the United States, shall consist only in levying War against them, or in adhering to their Enemies, giving them Aid and Comfort. No Person shall be convicted of Treason unless on the Testimony of two Witnesses to the same overt Act, or on Confession in open Court.

The Congress shall have Power to declare the Punishment of Treason, but no Attainder of Treason shall work Corruption of Blood, or Forfeiture except during the Life of the Person attainted.

Article. IV.

Section. 1.

Full Faith and Credit shall be given in each State to the public Acts, Records, and judicial Proceedings of every other State. And the

copyright 2016 © J. M. Payne

Congress may by general Laws prescribe the Manner in which such Acts, Records and Proceedings shall be proved, and the Effect thereof.

Section. 2.

The Citizens of each State shall be entitled to all Privileges and Immunities of Citizens in the several States.

A Person charged in any State with Treason, Felony, or other Crime, who shall flee from Justice, and be found in another State, shall on Demand of the executive Authority of the State from which he fled, be delivered up, to be removed to the State having Jurisdiction of the Crime.

No Person held to Service or Labour in one State, under the Laws thereof, escaping into another, shall, in Consequence of any Law or Regulation therein, be discharged from such Service or Labour, but shall be delivered up on Claim of the Party to whom such Service or Labour may be due.

Section. 3.

New States may be admitted by the Congress into this Union; but no new State shall be formed or erected within the Jurisdiction of any other State; nor any State be formed by the Junction of two or more States, or Parts of States, without the Consent of the Legislatures of the States concerned as well as of the Congress.

The Congress shall have Power to dispose of and make all needful Rules and Regulations respecting the Territory or other Property belonging to the United States; and nothing in this Constitution shall be so construed as to Prejudice any Claims of the United States, or of any particular State.

Section. 4.

The United States shall guarantee to every State in this Union a Republican Form of Government, and shall protect each of them against Invasion; and on Application of the Legislature, or of the Executive (when the Legislature cannot be convened), against domestic Violence.

Article. V.

The Congress, whenever two thirds of both Houses shall deem it necessary, shall propose Amendments to this Constitution, or, on the Application of the Legislatures of two thirds of the several States, shall call a Convention for proposing Amendments, which, in either Case, shall be valid to all Intents and Purposes, as Part of this Constitution, when ratified by the Legislatures of three fourths of the several States,

copyright © 2016 J. M. Payne

or by Conventions in three fourths thereof, as the one or the other Mode of Ratification may be proposed by the Congress; Provided that no Amendment which may be made prior to the Year One thousand eight hundred and eight shall in any Manner affect the first and fourth Clauses in the Ninth Section of the first Article; and that no State, without its Consent, shall be deprived of its equal Suffrage in the Senate.

Article. VI.

All Debts contracted and Engagements entered into, before the Adoption of this Constitution, shall be as valid against the United States under this Constitution, as under the Confederation.

This Constitution, and the Laws of the United States which shall be made in Pursuance thereof; and all Treaties made, or which shall be made, under the Authority of the United States, shall be the supreme Law of the Land; and the Judges in every State shall be bound thereby, any Thing in the Constitution or Laws of any State to the Contrary notwithstanding.

The Senators and Representatives before mentioned, and the Members of the several State Legislatures, and all executive and judicial Officers, both of the United States and of the several States, shall be bound by Oath or Affirmation, to support this Constitution; but no religious Test shall ever be required as a Qualification to any Office or public Trust under the United States.

Article. VII.

The Ratification of the Conventions of nine States, shall be sufficient for the Establishment of this Constitution between the States so ratifying the Same.

The Word, "the," being interlined between the seventh and eighth Lines of the first Page, the Word "Thirty" being partly written on an Erazure in the fifteenth Line of the first Page, The Words "is tried" being interlined between the thirty second and thirty third Lines of the first Page and the Word "the" being interlined between the forty third and forty fourth Lines of the second Page.

Attest William Jackson Secretary

done in Convention by the Unanimous Consent of the States present the Seventeenth Day of September in the Year of our Lord one thousand seven hundred and Eighty seven and of the Independance of the United States of America the Twelfth In witness whereof We have hereunto subscribed our Names,

copyright 2016 © J. M. Payne

G°. Washington
Presidt and deputy from Virginia

Delaware
Geo: Read
Gunning Bedford jun
John Dickinson
Richard Bassett
Jaco: Broom

New Hampshire
John Langdon
Nicholas Gilman

Maryland
James McHenry
Dan of St Thos. Jenifer
Danl. Carroll

Massachusetts
Nathaniel Gorham
Rufus King

Virginia
John Blair
James Madison Jr.

Connecticut
Wm. Saml. Johnson
Roger Sherman

North Carolina
Wm. Blount
Richd. Dobbs Spaight
Hu Williamson

New York
Alexander Hamilton

South Carolina
J. Rutledge
Charles Cotesworth Pinckney
Charles Pinckney
Pierce Butler

New Jersey
Wil: Livingston
David Brearley
Wm. Paterson
Jona: Dayton

Georgia
William Few
Abr Baldwin

Pennsylvania
B Franklin
Thomas Mifflin
Robt. Morris
Geo. Clymer
Thos. FitzSimons
Jared Ingersoll
James Wilson
Gouv Morris

The Preamble to The Bill of Rights

Congress of the United States
begun and held at the City of New-York, on

copyright © 2016 J. M. Payne

Wednesday the fourth of March, one thousand seven hundred and eighty nine.

THE Conventions of a number of the States, having at the time of their adopting the Constitution, expressed a desire, in order to prevent misconstruction or abuse of its powers, that further declaratory and restrictive clauses should be added: And as extending the ground of public confidence in the Government, will best ensure the beneficent ends of its institution.

RESOLVED by the Senate and House of Representatives of the United States of America, in Congress assembled, two thirds of both Houses concurring, that the following Articles be proposed to the Legislatures of the several States, as amendments to the Constitution of the United States, all, or any of which Articles, when ratified by three fourths of the said Legislatures, to be valid to all intents and purposes, as part of the said Constitution; viz.

ARTICLES in addition to, and Amendment of the Constitution of the United States of America, proposed by Congress, and ratified by the Legislatures of the several States, pursuant to the fifth Article of the original Constitution.

Amendment I

Congress shall make no law respecting an establishment of religion, or prohibiting the free exercise thereof; or abridging the freedom of speech, or of the press; or the right of the people peaceably to assemble, and to petition the Government for a redress of grievances.

Amendment II

A well regulated Militia, being necessary to the security of a free State, the right of the people to keep and bear Arms, shall not be infringed.

Amendment III

No Soldier shall, in time of peace be quartered in any house, without the consent of the Owner, nor in time of war, but in a manner to be prescribed by law.

Amendment IV

The right of the people to be secure in their persons, houses, papers, and effects, against unreasonable searches and seizures, shall not be violated, and no Warrants shall issue, but upon probable cause, supported by Oath or affirmation, and particularly describing the place to be searched, and the persons or things to be seized.

Amendment V

copyright 2016 © J. M. Payne

No person shall be held to answer for a capital, or otherwise infamous crime, unless on a presentment or indictment of a Grand Jury, except in cases arising in the land or naval forces, or in the Militia, when in actual service in time of War or public danger; nor shall any person be subject for the same offence to be twice put in jeopardy of life or limb; nor shall be compelled in any criminal case to be a witness against himself, nor be deprived of life, liberty, or property, without due process of law; nor shall private property be taken for public use, without just compensation.

Amendment VI

In all criminal prosecutions, the accused shall enjoy the right to a speedy and public trial, by an impartial jury of the State and district wherein the crime shall have been committed, which district shall have been previously ascertained by law, and to be informed of the nature and cause of the accusation; to be confronted with the witnesses against him; to have compulsory process for obtaining witnesses in his favor, and to have the Assistance of Counsel for his defence.

Amendment VII

In Suits at common law, where the value in controversy shall exceed twenty dollars, the right of trial by jury shall be preserved, and no fact tried by a jury, shall be otherwise re-examined in any Court of the United States, than according to the rules of the common law.

Amendment VIII

Excessive bail shall not be required, nor excessive fines imposed, nor cruel and unusual punishments inflicted.

Amendment IX

The enumeration in the Constitution, of certain rights, shall not be construed to deny or disparage others retained by the people.

Amendment X

The powers not delegated to the United States by the Constitution, nor prohibited by it to the States, are reserved to the States respectively, or to the people.

AMENDMENT XI

Passed by Congress March 4, 1794. Ratified February 7, 1795.

Note: Article III, section 2, of the Constitution was modified by amendment 11.

copyright © 2016 J. M. Payne

The Judicial power of the United States shall not be construed to extend to any suit in law or equity, commenced or prosecuted against one of the United States by Citizens of another State, or by Citizens or Subjects of any Foreign State.

AMENDMENT XII

Passed by Congress December 9, 1803. Ratified June 15, 1804.

Note: A portion of Article II, section 1 of the Constitution was superseded by the 12th amendment.

The Electors shall meet in their respective states and vote by ballot for President and Vice-President, one of whom, at least, shall not be an inhabitant of the same state with themselves; they shall name in their ballots the person voted for as President, and in distinct ballots the person voted for as Vice-President, and they shall make distinct lists of all persons voted for as President, and of all persons voted for as Vice-President, and of the number of votes for each, which lists they shall sign and certify, and transmit sealed to the seat of the government of the United States, directed to the President of the Senate; -- the President of the Senate shall, in the presence of the Senate and House of Representatives, open all the certificates and the votes shall then be counted; -- The person having the greatest number of votes for President, shall be the President, if such number be a majority of the whole number of Electors appointed; and if no person have such majority, then from the persons having the highest numbers not exceeding three on the list of those voted for as President, the House of Representatives shall choose immediately, by ballot, the President. But in choosing the President, the votes shall be taken by states, the representation from each state having one vote; a quorum for this purpose shall consist of a member or members from two-thirds of the states, and a majority of all the states shall be necessary to a choice. [And if the House of Representatives shall not choose a President whenever the right of choice shall devolve upon them, before the fourth day of March next following, then the Vice-President shall act as President, as in case of the death or other constitutional disability of the President. --]* The person having the greatest number of votes as Vice-President, shall be the Vice-President, if such number be a majority of the whole number of Electors appointed, and if no person have a majority, then from the two highest numbers on the list, the Senate shall choose the Vice-President; a quorum for the purpose shall consist of two-thirds of the whole number of Senators, and a majority of the whole number shall be necessary to a choice. But no person constitutionally ineligible to the office of President shall be eligible to that of Vice-President of the United States.

copyright 2016 © J. M. Payne

*Superseded by section 3 of the 20th amendment.

AMENDMENT XIII

Passed by Congress January 31, 1865. Ratified December 6, 1865.

Note: A portion of Article IV, section 2, of the Constitution was superseded by the 13th amendment.

Section 1.
Neither slavery nor involuntary servitude, except as a punishment for crime whereof the party shall have been duly convicted, shall exist within the United States, or any place subject to their jurisdiction.

Section 2.
Congress shall have power to enforce this article by appropriate legislation.

AMENDMENT XIV

Passed by Congress June 13, 1866. Ratified July 9, 1868.

Note: Article I, section 2, of the Constitution was modified by section 2 of the 14th amendment.

Section 1.
All persons born or naturalized in the United States, and subject to the jurisdiction thereof, are citizens of the United States and of the State wherein they reside. No State shall make or enforce any law which shall abridge the privileges or immunities of citizens of the United States; nor shall any State deprive any person of life, liberty, or property, without due process of law; nor deny to any person within its jurisdiction the equal protection of the laws.

Section 2.
Representatives shall be apportioned among the several States according to their respective numbers, counting the whole number of persons in each State, excluding Indians not taxed. But when the right to vote at any election for the choice of electors for President and Vice-President of the United States, Representatives in Congress, the Executive and Judicial officers of a State, or the members of the Legislature thereof, is denied to any of the male inhabitants of such State, being twenty-one years of age,* and citizens of the United States, or in any way abridged, except for participation in rebellion, or other crime, the basis of representation therein shall be reduced in the proportion which the number of such male citizens shall bear to the whole number of male citizens twenty-one years of age in such State.

copyright © 2016 J. M. Payne

Section 3.
No person shall be a Senator or Representative in Congress, or elector of President and Vice-President, or hold any office, civil or military, under the United States, or under any State, who, having previously taken an oath, as a member of Congress, or as an officer of the United States, or as a member of any State legislature, or as an executive or judicial officer of any State, to support the Constitution of the United States, shall have engaged in insurrection or rebellion against the same, or given aid or comfort to the enemies thereof. But Congress may by a vote of two-thirds of each House, remove such disability.

Section 4.
The validity of the public debt of the United States, authorized by law, including debts incurred for payment of pensions and bounties for services in suppressing insurrection or rebellion, shall not be questioned. But neither the United States nor any State shall assume or pay any debt or obligation incurred in aid of insurrection or rebellion against the United States, or any claim for the loss or emancipation of any slave; but all such debts, obligations and claims shall be held illegal and void.

Section 5.
The Congress shall have the power to enforce, by appropriate legislation, the provisions of this article.

*Changed by section 1 of the 26th amendment.

AMENDMENT XV

Passed by Congress February 26, 1869. Ratified February 3, 1870.

Section 1.
The right of citizens of the United States to vote shall not be denied or abridged by the United States or by any State on account of race, color, or previous condition of servitude--

Section 2.
The Congress shall have the power to enforce this article by appropriate legislation.

AMENDMENT XVI

Passed by Congress July 2, 1909. Ratified February 3, 1913.

Note: Article I, section 9, of the Constitution was modified by amendment 16.

copyright 2016 © J. M. Payne

The Congress shall have power to lay and collect taxes on incomes, from whatever source derived, without apportionment among the several States, and without regard to any census or enumeration.

AMENDMENT XVII

Passed by Congress May 13, 1912. Ratified April 8, 1913.

Note: Article I, section 3, of the Constitution was modified by the 17th amendment.

The Senate of the United States shall be composed of two Senators from each State, elected by the people thereof, for six years; and each Senator shall have one vote. The electors in each State shall have the qualifications requisite for electors of the most numerous branch of the State legislatures.

When vacancies happen in the representation of any State in the Senate, the executive authority of such State shall issue writs of election to fill such vacancies: Provided, That the legislature of any State may empower the executive thereof to make temporary appointments until the people fill the vacancies by election as the legislature may direct.

This amendment shall not be so construed as to affect the election or term of any Senator chosen before it becomes valid as part of the Constitution.

AMENDMENT XVIII

Passed by Congress December 18, 1917. Ratified January 16, 1919. Repealed by amendment 21.

Section 1.
After one year from the ratification of this article the manufacture, sale, or transportation of intoxicating liquors within, the importation thereof into, or the exportation thereof from the United States and all territory subject to the jurisdiction thereof for beverage purposes is hereby prohibited.

Section 2.
The Congress and the several States shall have concurrent power to enforce this article by appropriate legislation.

Section 3.
This article shall be inoperative unless it shall have been ratified as an amendment to the Constitution by the legislatures of the several States, as provided in the Constitution, within seven years from the date of the submission hereof to the States by the Congress.

copyright © 2016 J. M. Payne

AMENDMENT XIX

Passed by Congress June 4, 1919. Ratified August 18, 1920.

The right of citizens of the United States to vote shall not be denied or abridged by the United States or by any State on account of sex.

Congress shall have power to enforce this article by appropriate legislation.

AMENDMENT XX

Passed by Congress March 2, 1932. Ratified January 23, 1933.

Note: Article I, section 4, of the Constitution was modified by section 2 of this amendment. In addition, a portion of the 12th amendment was superseded by section 3.

Section 1.
The terms of the President and the Vice President shall end at noon on the 20th day of January, and the terms of Senators and Representatives at noon on the 3rd day of January, of the years in which such terms would have ended if this article had not been ratified; and the terms of their successors shall then begin.

Section 2.
The Congress shall assemble at least once in every year, and such meeting shall begin at noon on the 3d day of January, unless they shall by law appoint a different day.

Section 3.
If, at the time fixed for the beginning of the term of the President, the President elect shall have died, the Vice President elect shall become President. If a President shall not have been chosen before the time fixed for the beginning of his term, or if the President elect shall have failed to qualify, then the Vice President elect shall act as President until a President shall have qualified; and the Congress may by law provide for the case wherein neither a President elect nor a Vice President shall have qualified, declaring who shall then act as President, or the manner in which one who is to act shall be selected, and such person shall act accordingly until a President or Vice President shall have qualified.

Section 4.
The Congress may by law provide for the case of the death of any of the persons from whom the House of Representatives may choose a President whenever the right of choice shall have devolved upon them, and for the case of the death of any of the persons from whom the

copyright 2016 © J. M. Payne

Senate may choose a Vice President whenever the right of choice shall have devolved upon them.

Section 5.
Sections 1 and 2 shall take effect on the 15th day of October following the ratification of this article.

Section 6.
This article shall be inoperative unless it shall have been ratified as an amendment to the Constitution by the legislatures of three-fourths of the several States within seven years from the date of its submission.

AMENDMENT XXI

Passed by Congress February 20, 1933. Ratified December 5, 1933.

Section 1.
The eighteenth article of amendment to the Constitution of the United States is hereby repealed.

Section 2.
The transportation or importation into any State, Territory, or Possession of the United States for delivery or use therein of intoxicating liquors, in violation of the laws thereof, is hereby prohibited.

Section 3.
This article shall be inoperative unless it shall have been ratified as an amendment to the Constitution by conventions in the several States, as provided in the Constitution, within seven years from the date of the submission hereof to the States by the Congress.

AMENDMENT XXII

Passed by Congress March 21, 1947. Ratified February 27, 1951.

Section 1.
No person shall be elected to the office of the President more than twice, and no person who has held the office of President, or acted as President, for more than two years of a term to which some other person was elected President shall be elected to the office of President more than once. But this Article shall not apply to any person holding the office of President when this Article was proposed by Congress, and shall not prevent any person who may be holding the office of President, or acting as President, during the term within which this Article becomes operative from holding the office of President or acting as President during the remainder of such term.

copyright © 2016 J. M. Payne

Section 2.
This article shall be inoperative unless it shall have been ratified as an amendment to the Constitution by the legislatures of three-fourths of the several States within seven years from the date of its submission to the States by the Congress.

AMENDMENT XXIII

Passed by Congress June 16, 1960. Ratified March 29, 1961.

Section 1.
The District constituting the seat of Government of the United States shall appoint in such manner as Congress may direct:

A number of electors of President and Vice President equal to the whole number of Senators and Representatives in Congress to which the District would be entitled if it were a State, but in no event more than the least populous State; they shall be in addition to those appointed by the States, but they shall be considered, for the purposes of the election of President and Vice President, to be electors appointed by a State; and they shall meet in the District and perform such duties as provided by the twelfth article of amendment.

Section 2.
The Congress shall have power to enforce this article by appropriate legislation.

AMENDMENT XXIV

Passed by Congress August 27, 1962. Ratified January 23, 1964.

Section 1.
The right of citizens of the United States to vote in any primary or other election for President or Vice President, for electors for President or Vice President, or for Senator or Representative in Congress, shall not be denied or abridged by the United States or any State by reason of failure to pay poll tax or other tax.

Section 2.
The Congress shall have power to enforce this article by appropriate legislation.

AMENDMENT XXV

Passed by Congress July 6, 1965. Ratified February 10, 1967.

Note: Article II, section 1, of the Constitution was affected by the 25th amendment.

copyright 2016 © J. M. Payne

Section 1.

In case of the removal of the President from office or of his death or resignation, the Vice President shall become President.

Section 2.

Whenever there is a vacancy in the office of the Vice President, the President shall nominate a Vice President who shall take office upon confirmation by a majority vote of both Houses of Congress.

Section 3.

Whenever the President transmits to the President pro tempore of the Senate and the Speaker of the House of Representatives his written declaration that he is unable to discharge the powers and duties of his office, and until he transmits to them a written declaration to the contrary, such powers and duties shall be discharged by the Vice President as Acting President.

Section 4.

Whenever the Vice President and a majority of either the principal officers of the executive departments or of such other body as Congress may by law provide, transmit to the President pro tempore of the Senate and the Speaker of the House of Representatives their written declaration that the President is unable to discharge the powers and duties of his office, the Vice President shall immediately assume the powers and duties of the office as Acting President.

Thereafter, when the President transmits to the President pro tempore of the Senate and the Speaker of the House of Representatives his written declaration that no inability exists, he shall resume the powers and duties of his office unless the Vice President and a majority of either the principal officers of the executive department or of such other body as Congress may by law provide, transmit within four days to the President pro tempore of the Senate and the Speaker of the House of Representatives their written declaration that the President is unable to discharge the powers and duties of his office. Thereupon Congress shall decide the issue, assembling within forty-eight hours for that purpose if not in session. If the Congress, within twenty-one days after receipt of the latter written declaration, or, if Congress is not in session, within twenty-one days after Congress is required to assemble, determines by two-thirds vote of both Houses that the President is unable to discharge the powers and duties of his office, the Vice President shall continue to discharge the same as Acting President; otherwise, the President shall resume the powers and duties of his office.

AMENDMENT XXVI

copyright © 2016 J. M. Payne

Passed by Congress March 23, 1971. Ratified July 1, 1971.

Note: Amendment 14, section 2, of the Constitution was modified by section 1 of the 26th amendment.

Section 1.
The right of citizens of the United States, who are eighteen years of age or older, to vote shall not be denied or abridged by the United States or by any State on account of age.

Section 2.
The Congress shall have power to enforce this article by appropriate legislation.

AMENDMENT XXVII

Originally proposed Sept. 25, 1789. Ratified May 7, 1992.

No law, varying the compensation for the services of the Senators and Representatives, shall take effect, until an election of representatives shall have intervened.

copyright 2016 © J. M. Payne

BIBLIOGRAPHY & SUGGESTED READING:

Books:

"Setting the Record Straight: American History in Black & White", David Barton -- race & politics

"Animal Farm", George Orwell -- tyranny

"Atlas Shrugged", Ayn Rand -- socio-economic systems

"The Bible", God -- everything

"Common Sense", Thomas Paine

"The Crisis", Thomas Paine -- American Founding

"The Debate on the Constitution", the American Founders -- the Constitution

"Democracy in America", Alexis de Tocqueville -- social system

"Demographic Winter: the Decline of the Human Family", Judith Adolphson & Rick Stout -- family & society

"Dumbing Us Down", John Taylor Gatto -- schools

"The Forgotten Ways: Reactivating the Missional Church" Frank Viola -- Christian community

"The Forgotten Man", Amity Schlaes -- the economy

"The Forgotten Ways", Alan Hirsch -- Christian community

"Friends in High Places", William L. Livingston -- socio-technical systems

"Have Fun at Work", William L. Livingston -- socio-technical systems

"An Inconvenient Book", Glenn Beck -- socio-political systems

"Let Freedom Ring: Winning the War of Liberty over Liberalism", Sean Hannity -- politics

"The Law", Frederic Bastiat -- political systems

"The Liberty Amendments", Mark Levin -- the Constitution

"Men in Black", Mark Levin -- the judicial system

"The Narrative of Frederick Douglass an American Slave", Frederick Douglass -- slavery

copyright © 2016 J. M. Payne

"Plain, Honest Men: The Making of the American Constitution", Richard Beeman -- the Constitutional Convention

"Rules for Radicals", Saul Alinski -- Liberal tactics

"Second Treatise of Government", John Locke -- political systems

"See I Told You So", Rush Limbaugh -- politics

"A Step Farther Out", Jerry Pournelle -- technology

"The Tangible Kingdom: Creating Incarnational Community", Hugh Halter & Matt Smay -- community

"Tempest at Dawn", James D. Best -- the Constitutional Convention

"Thoughts on Government", John Adams -- government

"The Way Things Ought to Be", Rush Limbaugh -- politics

Websites:

avalon.law.yale.edu - historical documents

www.archives.gov/exhibits/charters/ -- founding documents

www.americanthinker.com - politics

www.articlevcaucus.com - Article 5 Convention

www.biblestudytools.com - Bible study assistance

www.billwhittle.com - socio-politico-technical commentary

www.breitbart.com - political news

www.conventionofstates.com - Article 5 Convention

coolidgeproject.us - restoring federalism

frankviola.org - Christian community

http://www.nasa.gov/mission_pages/Mini-RF/multimedia/feature_ice_like_deposits.html - Water on the Moon

pjmedia.com - political news

http://www.popularmechanics.com/science/space/deep/4201569 - dodging the asteroid Apophis

www.powerlineblog.com - political news

www.realclearpolitics.com - political news

spectator.org - politics

copyright 2016 © J. M. Payne

townhall.com - politics

www.theforgottenways.org - Christian community

www.usfirst.org - youth robotics competition

www.wallbuilders.com - American history

J. M. Payne is that rarity, a native Floridian. He was able to persuade one woman to marry him & is the adoptive father of three children. He is follower of Jesus, though not very good at it. As an engineer with a career at a major defense contractor, he understands the dysfunctional interface between reality & government. A life-long Conservative, he votes Republican, though he often has to hold his nose to do so.

copyright © 2016 J. M. Payne

www.ingramcontent.com/pod-product-compliance
Lightning Source LLC
Chambersburg PA
CBHW072102280526

45788CB00006B/2363